Self-Esteem: A Classroom Affair
Volume 2

More Ways to Help Children
Like Themselves

Michele and Craig Borba

Winston Press, Inc.   430 Oak Grove   Minneapolis, MN 55403

Developmental, editorial, design, and
production services:
Canning Mulvehill Productions, Inc.
Design: Nancy Arend
Illustrations: Marcia Allard Sheppleman

Library of Congress Catalog Card Number: 80-53554
ISBN: 0-86683-675-6

5   4   3   2   1

Winston Press, Inc.
430 Oak Grove
Minneapolis, MN 55403

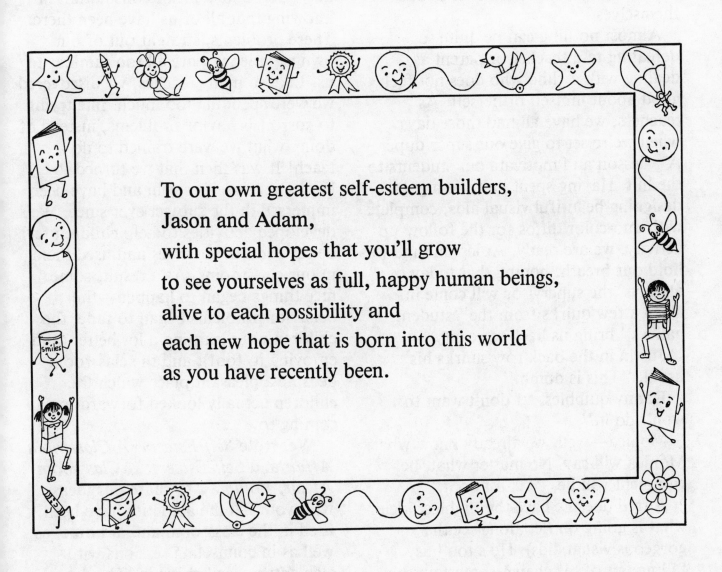

To our own greatest self-esteem builders,
Jason and Adam,
with special hopes that you'll grow
to see yourselves as full, happy human beings,
alive to each possibility and
each new hope that is born into this world
as you have recently been.

PREFACE

By picking up this book, you've revealed that, like us, you are interested in helping children feel better about themselves.

Almost nothing can be quite so defeating to a teacher or parent as dealing with a child who does not feel good about himself or herself. As teachers, we have all had those days when we're set to give our super-duper, A+ lesson and motivate our students to the hilt. Having spent half the night designing beautiful visual aids, complete with duo-color dittos for the follow-up activity, we are ready. At lesson time we hold our breath, hoping that today of all days, the supervisor will come in. Then a few quirks from the "student gallery" bring us back to reality.

Justin in the back row smirks his usual, "This is dumb."

Danny quibbles, "I don't want to... won't do it."

Monica—well, we already know what Monica will say. No matter what, her comment will be, "I can't do it."

Alfred doesn't have the slightest idea what is going on (let alone see the gorgeous visual aids). He's too busy falling out of his chair to entertain the children around him.

Sound familiar? If you can call on your reserve energies to get behind the aggressive, defeatest, and clowning disguises, you'll probably discover that all of these children suffer from the same disease—low self-image. It's a common classroom ailment. And judging from the comments made in the teachers' room, it seems rampant.

Unfortunately, no cure-all innoculation exists. So what can you do? First, take a bit of consolation in knowing that all of us have been there. These problems, straight out of our own experiences, are all too familiar to us. Like so many teaches, we discovered we were spending too much time trying to correct behavior problems, instead of doing what we were trained to do—teach! It was then that we turned to books about self-esteem and have been immersed in the subject ever since. We developed activities to help children feel better about themselves and used them in our classrooms. As a result, some nice things began to happen—the behavior problems began to fade; the children were learning a lot better (and enjoying it, too!); and the classroom became a pleasant place which the children actually looked forward to coming to.

We wrote *Self-Esteem: A Classroom Affair* and *Self-Esteem: A Classroom Affair, Volume 2* to share our ideas with you. All the activities have been used in the classroom and at home, as well as in counseling sessions with elementary-aged children. They've certainly enhanced our environments and we hope they enrich yours. We welcome the opportunity to conduct in-service training sessions to present our ideas and activities to teachers and leaders interested in affective child development.

Happy Enhancing!
Michele and Craig Borba

CONTENTS

Introduction
THE EMERGING SELF

The secret of education lies in respecting the pupil.

Ralph Waldo Emerson

THE FORMATION OF SELF

Adults once viewed children as blank slates with few worthwhile qualities. But research and reason have proven this perception false. We now know that even very young children have more complex and sophisticated cognitive and emotional capabilities than were previously imagined.

Research has also revealed that children begin to mold their self-images at a very young age and that positive, successful experiences enhance the formation of a positive self-image in the crucial early years. By creating environments in which children can feel secure about themselves and have many opportunities to develop their strengths, parents and teachers can help children have those positive experiences. This is what *Self-Esteem: A Classroom Affair, Volume 2* is all about—providing activities to help children be self-enhanced.

THE DEVELOPMENT OF SELF-IMAGE

The inner picture each of us has of ourself defines how we see ourselves as persons and how we think other people see us. This inner picture, or self-image, affects how we act and think.

Research psychologists have documented these interesting facts about self-image:

- self-image is acquired, not inherited;
- self-image guides thinking and behavior;
- self-image affects creativity, integrity, stability;
- self-image plays a role in the kind of friends, the type of job, and the spouse a person chooses.

A newborn baby does not know of its existence as a unique and separate entity. Yet it is not long thereafter that a child begins to accumulate experiences and develop a self-image. Each new experience helps a child organize and reorganize his or her sense of self.

The people a child deems as worthy and important—the child's significant others—have a great impact on the formation of the child's "inner picture of self."

The repeated behavior of significant others helps mold the child's image of self. So it is important to realize that significant others can have both positive and negative effects on a child's self-image formation. A child whose experiences are good and who is accepted unconditionally as a significant being will begin to grow as a person. The child will begin to picture himself or herself as a wanted, loved, valued, worthy being, because the significant people in his or her life are painting such a picture.

"What a nice baby!"
"You're so much fun to be with!"
"Daddy and Mommy love you so much!"
"What a good baby you are!"

Significant others can also have a devastating effect on a child's self-image formation. A child who hears nothing but negative, degrading comments begins to believe he or she is unworthy, unloved, and valueless.

"Why do you always make such messes?"
"You're so naughty all the time."
"I know you're not going to be good, so why should I take you anywhere with me?"
"You're such a pain to be around."
"Can't you ever do anything right?"

COOPERSMITH'S FINDINGS

Stanley Coopersmith, a child psychologist at the University of California at Davis, has devoted his life to the study of self-image. His book *The Antecedents of Self-Esteem* has become a landmark research work in the area of self-esteem. Dr. Coopersmith studied over 1,700 boys and their families. His findings reveal that these boys' attitudes about themselves were formed by how their parents or significant others saw them or on how the boys thought they were seen by parents and significant others.

Coopersmith's study also revealed that the self-confident and successful young men had these three things in common.

1. They came from loving homes where they experienced the kind of love that expresses respect and concern and that helps a child feel like a significant being, worthy of interest and pride.
2. Their parents were significantly less permissive than were the parents of children with lower self-esteem.
3. Their families showed a high degree of democracy. The children were encouraged to present their own ideas and opinions for discussion (even those that did not agree with the ideas and opinions of their parents).

As a result of his research, Coopersmith developed a list of characteristics that may help parents and teachers pinpoint children with low self-esteem.

Fearful and Timid   This child is quite insecure about new undertakings and is very uncomfortable in social settings. While insecurity is quite normal in very young children, children who do not outgrow this tendency provide cause for concern.

Bullying and Bragging   Quite often teachers and parents neglect to consider that low self-esteem could be the root of the bully and braggart's behavior. In fact, this child is often mistakenly thought of as having too much self-esteem. Dr. Coopersmith warns us not to be fooled; this child may actually be masking a weak, soft center and his or her true inner feelings with a tough, outer disguise.

Unable to Make Decisions   This child, who never seems able to make up his or her mind, may have had past decisions continually rebuked and ridiculed or may have role models who vacilate themselves.

Expects Failure   This child (and we've all known him or her at one time or another) greets every activity—no matter what it is—with comments like "I can't do that" or "It's too hard." This child's expectations of failure may stem from an established pattern begun by the child to gain extra attention or as the result of a series of failures.

Reluctant to Express Opinions   This child presents a passive personality and seems uninterested in the world around him or her. Don't be fooled; this child may well have an opinion, but be unwilling or unable to express it.

These characteristics are warning signals and should not be used as the final determiners of low self-esteem. More important than using the presence of these symptoms to diagnose, often incorrectly, that a child has low self-esteem is for parents and teachers to ask themselves:

- Why is the child acting this way?
- Could it be that this child is not feeling good about himself or herself?
- What can I do to help this child feel better about himself or herself?

THE COMPONENTS OF SELF-ESTEEM

As a child grows and has more experiences, his or her inner picture of self expands. Experiences of the "physical self," the "thinking self," and the "social self" all help mold the child's self-image.

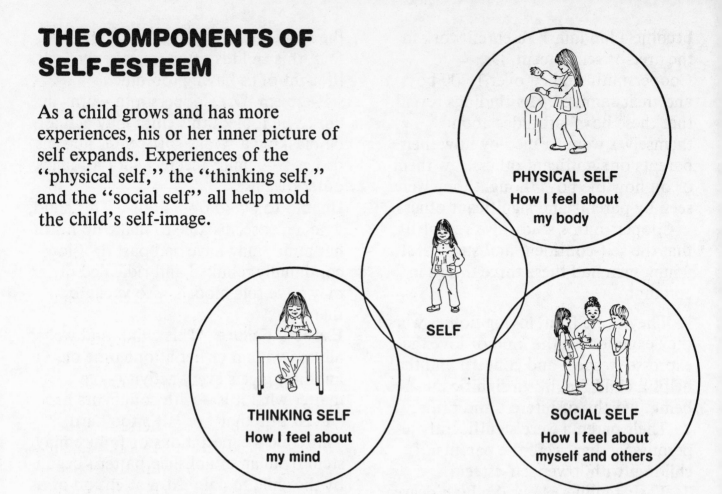

PHYSICAL SELF
How I feel about my body

SELF

THINKING SELF
How I feel about my mind

SOCIAL SELF
How I feel about myself and others

Physical Self   Involves the appearance and performance of a child's body. A child with successful physical-self experiences might make comments like these:

"I have such nice printing."
"May I join the soccer team?"
"Everyone says I look nice in my new outfit."
"I'm getting to be so good at jumping rope."

A child having unsuccessful physical experiences might say:

"I hate recess; there's never anything to do."
"I don't want to take my coat off; I'm too ugly."
"Why did you buy me this ball? I'm no good with it anyway."

Thinking Self   Involves what a child knows—the basic concepts in reading, writing, and arithmetic taught in school each day. Positive thinking self-images will produce statements like these:

"I'm such a smart boy."
"This math is easy."
"I learn fast."
"I like to read."

Experiences of failure for the thinking self produce these kinds of statements:

"I'm so dumb."
"Why can't I learn like everyone else?"
"I hate school; it's too hard."
"I don't want to read again."

4

Social Self Involves a child's relationships with others—family members, classmates, peers, acquaintances, and so on. A child who feels good about his or her social experiences might say:

"Can Johnny come over to play?"
"I like being with my family."
"I sure have a lot of good friends."
"Everybody likes me."
"School is a fun place to be; all my friends are there."

A child who's social self is having negative experiences might say:

"Why do I have to go to school? Nobody likes me."
"There's never anyone to play with."
"I don't want to go with you on a vacation; there's never anything to do."
"Do I have to talk to her? She won't like me anyway."

Positive experiences in each of the self-image components enhance a child's total self-image; negative experiences diminish it. *Self-Esteem: A Classroom Affair, Volume 2* seeks to provide many positive experiences in each of the self-image components and to help teachers be sensitive to each child's sense of self, so that they can help children improve their opinions of themselves.

SOCIAL INTERACTIONS

It's evident that young children come to school with preconceived ideas about themselves and their abilities. Preschool experiences have contributed to their sense of value as human beings, as well as to their ability to cope successfully with the environment.

The child psychologist Jean Piaget has opened the eyes of child caregivers with his brilliant descriptions of the capabilities of young children. He has helped us recognize that the young child is busy forming the concept "Me" and "Who I am in relationship to the world." Piaget describes this behavior as *egocentric* in that the child literally sees himself or herself as the center of the universe. As a result, the young child, not yet aware that not everyone thinks and feels as he or she does, is incapable of putting himself or herself in another's shoes.

It is only gradually that children move out of this egocentric state and into the new level of sociocentricity. Through good relationships and experiences, social cooperation begins to emerge. With successful social interactions, children gradually begin to develop the capability of perceiving another person's point of view.

Certainly the discovery of friends is a major step in a child's acquisition of social knowledge. Before friends become part of a child's world, his or her major relationships consist primarily of family members, particularly parents and siblings. As the child moves out of this close inner circle, he or she begins to experience new types of social interactions not usually possible within the family structure.

The first day of school is a milestone in the lives of all children. They begin to learn basic socialization functions—some pleasant and some unpleasant, but all part of growing with others. They learn, for instance, that they may not always be accepted and must develop a repertoire of "give and take" to succeed within their peer structure.

Children are ever engaged in a struggle for social recognition and peers can provide important avenues for social development that adults cannot. Through friendships, children can enter into an interaction of mutual affiliation. They can share problems, joys, and experiences with others of the same age. They can also learn to relate to others as equals.

As with the other components of self-image, the social self requires many positive successes in order for a child to feel secure about his or her relationships. Many successful experiences with peers are necessary if a child is to develop a positive social self-picture.

Self-Esteem: A Classroom Affair, Volume 2 devotes several chapters to activities designed to provide opportunities for children to experience successful peer interactions within their own classroom. These activities will serve as a starting point from which many other peer interactions will grow.

BUILDING SELF-ESTEEM IN THE CLASSROOM

Research tells us that teachers can be significant others to the children they come in contact with. Thus, they can have a significant impact, both positive and negative, on children's formation of self-image.

Teachers can also help children change poor self-images, seemingly at any age, but in so doing should keep in mind these important points.

- Helping a child improve a poor self-image is not easy, nor does change occur over night. Change takes place very slowly.
- Consistency is very important. The teacher must be willing to make a conscious effort each day to help the child develop more positive feelings about himself or herself.
- The teacher's attitude and the classroom environment play significant roles in helping a child form a more positive self-picture.

THE TEACHER'S ATTITUDE

A teacher becomes a child's significant other when the child values the teacher as a person and when the child feels he or she is a significant being to the teacher. It is important, then, that the teacher's attitude invite and nurture positive self-enhancement in the children he or she deals with. Since teachers' attitudes are controlled by their own feelings of competency and self-worth and by their feelings about the children they are working with, it is important that teachers periodically review their own self-pictures. A teacher who hopes to help a child improve his or her self-image should have these qualities:

- a genuine interest and concern for the child;
- a rapport with the child such that the child feels the teacher is a significant person to him or her;

- a genuine recognition of the positive qualities of the child;
- an understanding that the child feels very poorly about himself or herself;
- a real belief that the child's self-image can change;
- a willingness to make the effort and take the time to help the child feel better about himself or herself;
- the self-trust and self-respect to be confident that he or she can be instrumental in helping the child improve a poor self-image;
- the confidence to check and recheck his or her own standings before jumping to the conclusion that "a full moon," "too much sugar," or "too little sleep" is the reason for the child's behavior.

THE CLASSROOM ENVIRONMENT

The teacher, as significant other, must create an environment conducive to positive self-image building. Only when such an environment exists will specific self-esteem activities be effective. Even the most expensively-packaged kit with its many alternatives for self-esteem raising will be rendered useless by an improper environment.

Classrooms which promote positive self-image building can usually be described using these words:

- caring
- open
- nonthreatening
- trusting
- involving
- nonjudgmental
- secure
- nurturing
- accepting
- encouraging
- kid-oriented
- inviting
- warm
- happy
- comfortable
- positive

7

Research has shown that environments that are most effective in enhancing self-esteem and improving self-image are those in which:

1. Children perceive a sense of warmth and love;
2. Children are offered a degree of security which allows them to grow and to try new things without an overriding concern about failure;
3. Children are respected as individuals;
4. Children's ideas and initiative are encouraged;
5. Children are invited to express opinions;
6. Children recognize that there are clear and definite limits within the environment;
7. Rules and standards are reasonably and consistently enforced;
8. Children have a chance to succeed at their own levels.

USING THIS BOOK

Self-Esteem: A Classroom Affair, Volume 2 provides a collection of ideas, activities, centers, and independent learning contracts to help enhance children's feelings of self-worth. The book can and should be used to fit *your* needs and the needs of *your students.* You may choose to use each suggestion—

*   with a large group *or* with small groups;
*   for the entire class *or* for individuals;
*   as an assignment *or* as a free-choice activity.

Several activities in this book call for the children to write their thoughts about a particular topic. You can adapt these activities for children who do not yet read and write by having them dictate their responses to you or to classroom helpers (older children, parents) and by having the children draw pictures to show their ideas on the backs of the written sheets.

The children will use large manipulatives for many of the activities in this book. You may wish to set up activity centers where the children can find and use the necessary materials and supplies when working on particular projects.

ESSENTIAL MATERIALS

In most cases, the activities in *Self-Esteem: A Classroom Affair, Volume 2* require the use of rather common materials and assume they are available in most classrooms. (Where less common materials are needed, they are listed or described near the beginning of the activity.) For your convenience you may wish to have an ample supply of the following materials available in your classroom and in special activity centers you set up.

- pencils
- crayons
- felt-tipped pens
- permanent markers
- paints
- paint brushes
- scissors
- paste or glue
- writing paper
- drawing paper
- wallpaper
- gift wrap
- construction paper
- decorating items: rickrack, lace, yarn, buttons, macaroni, seeds, glitter, assorted stickers
- material, felt, and construction-paper scraps

SOME LAST-MINUTE MENTIONABLES

(to read and reread, especially on those days when you wonder why you bothered to get that paper called a "teaching credential")

Remember—

1. Research shows that *you can change* self-esteem. This change can be positive or negative. As significant other, you determine which way the coin lands.

2. Situational specifics are possible— you can help a child with an unhappy home situation feel better about himself or herself at school.

3. The early years are the crucial ones for self-esteem building. It is during these years that you can do the most to help children feel good about themselves.

4. Change won't be easy—don't kid yourself, or expect too much too soon. Change takes place slowly. Be patient— it's worth it.

5. Provide as many opportunities for children to succeed as you can.

6. A positive attitude really is contagious! If children hear you consistently saying positive things to others in the room, they will begin to verbalize and feel the positive, too! In no time, they'll be passing it on to others.

7. All of us have our dark, dreary days. You can't always be a bubbly, positive, affective educator. Keep in mind that while you're in the business of boosting children's feelings about themselves, sometimes you can use some boosting, too. Finding other colleagues who share

your child-enhancing goals can be very helpful when those dark and dreary days do arrive.

8. It is essential that you work at creating an environment of mutual support and caring, a place where kids can feel secure and comfortable. Each day remind yourself of how important this is. Try to start out each day on a positive, happy note by deliberately greeting each child at the door with a caring statement. (We once heard a child psychologist talk about how important positive statements were. ''Each day it's important to try to point out one thing positive to each child— even if it means for a while that you tell a few children you like the way they brush their teeth.'') The important thing is that children begin to gain an awareness of who they are and what their strengths are so they can feel good about themselves.

9. And finally, remember above all that change comes through *you*. You are a significant other in your students' lives. You *can* help children feel better about themselves.

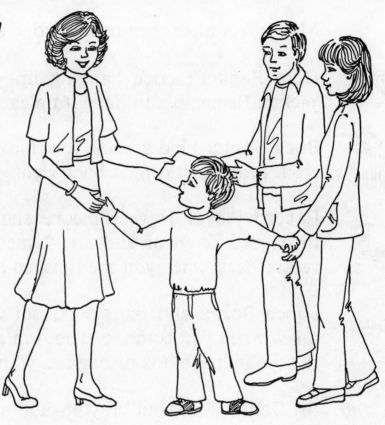

*We awaken in others
the same attitude of mind
we hold toward them.*

Elbert Hubbard

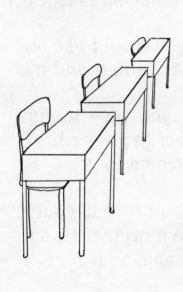

YOU AND I

There is no way we can overstate the importance of interpersonal relationships in our lives. Most of us mingle constantly with groups or individuals during the greater portion of each day. Our relationships take on different characteristics depending on the setting, be it school, business, home, or social. And one thing is for certain—we all find it easier to be part of a group that we feel good about being with. Our characters seem to change—we're more relaxed, comfortable, and open.

Children are really no different. They're forced to be parts of groups just as adults are. If the children in your class feel accepted by their peers and feel secure and comfortable in the setting, they'll want to be in your room.

The activities in this chapter will help children develop that initial feeling of "belongingness." The ideas and techniques will enhance children's awareness of others and help them develop their own interpersonal skills.

BACK-TO-SCHOOL CONTRACT

Name _____

Make an X after each task as you complete it.

 Coat Rack Practice hanging up your sweater or jacket. Remember to hang it up each time you take it off.

 Book Center Find a book you think you would like to read. Practice putting it back right where you found it.

 Record Player Have someone show you how to turn the record player on and off. Remember to put each record back when you are finished listening to it.

 Lunch Boxes and Bags Find out where to put your lunch when you come to school in the morning. Be sure that your lunch box or bag has your name on it.

 Art Center Take out crayons and a piece of paper. Draw a picture of something you did this summer. Then put everything back right where you found it.

 Bathrooms Find out where the girls' and boys' bathrooms are. Learn how to get back to your own classroom.

 Office Check to see where the office is and how to get there. Introduce yourself to the secretary and the principal. Remember that they are there to help you.

 Game Center Take a game out and look at all the pieces. Practice putting them back exactly as you found them. Then put the game away.

BEFORE THE BELL RINGS

To foster a feeling of belongingness and a spirit of togetherness, hold a Back-to-School Gathering. Send notes to all the children in your room. Introduce yourself; invite the children and their parents to the gathering; inform them of the date (either before school opens or on the first day of class), time, and room number; solicit parent help in providing refreshments; and ask each child to bring a recent snapshot of himself or herself.

As the children and their parents arrive, greet them with a big hello and give them name tags and a copy of the contract on page 12 (adapted to your needs and grade level). By completing the tasks described in the contract, each child can enjoy the day with his or her significant other as they explore the room and school together.

FIRST DAY JITTERS

The first day of school is a time of jitters for everyone, teachers and students alike. Here are a few ideas to start your year off on a happy and positive note.

HELLO BOARD

Ask the children to bring in small snapshots themselves, if they have not already done so in response to the request in your ''Before School'' letter. Cut out construction paper figures for the number of boys and girls in your class. Cut out a few extra figures for those ''opening day surprises'' (when an unexpected child or two appears at your door). Print the name of each child on an appropriate figure with black felt pen. Prepare a bulletin board with a brightly colored background. (Wallpaper and gift-wrapping paper provide good background themes.) Then pin the figures up so that they appear to be holding hands. Pin a caption such as ''Getting to Know You...Hoping You Like Me'' across the top of the board.

On the first day of school, at your ''Gathering,'' or sometime during the first week of the year have each child add his or her picture to the figure with his or her name on it. Children will go back to the board again and again to look at the pictures and to find out who's who.

SO YOU CAN'T REMEMBER WHO'S WHO

Opening days can be hectic—especially if you have a class of thirty youngsters and a poor memory for names and faces. The snapshots the children bring in can be lifesavers!

Tape the pictures lightly to a sheet of paper and write the names of the children under their pictures. Using a good copying machine, perhaps one that copies in color, make a dozen or more copies of the pictures.

Cut several sets of pictures apart. Paste each child's picture on his or her name tag, desk, cubbie, hanger, lunch-pail shelf—actually any place where you see the need. Put clear contact paper over the pictures to preserve them longer. Make an extra set of name tags with pictures for substitute teachers—they'll be forever thankful!

VALUABLE SCHOOL COUPONS

Duplicate enough of the coupons below so that each child in your class will have a copy of each coupon. (You may wish to make extra blank coupons to be filled in as appropriate occasions arise.)

Cut the coupons apart and staple them together with the cover on top to form coupon booklets. Distribute the booklets during the first day of school and watch the pleasant expressions emerge.

Cut along solid line.

VALUABLE SCHOOL COUPONS

You may sit next to the teacher at lunch one time.

Student _____

Teacher _____

Redeemable in Room _____

You may choose one book to be read during story time.

Student _____

Teacher _____

Redeemable in Room _____

You may choose one classroom chore to do.

Student _____

Teacher _____

Redeemable in Room _____

You may choose one game to be played during p.e. time.

Student _____

Teacher _____

Redeemable in Room _____

You may _____

_____

Student _____

Teacher _____

You must negotiate the value of this coupon with your teacher.

HAPPY THOUGHTS MAKE HAPPY KIDS

Sometime during the first day, you'll certainly want to let the children know your expectations and your class rules. One of the most important rules will probably be: "If you can't say something nice, don't say anything at all." Talk with the class about the meaning of this quote and how it affects your classroom. At the end of the discussion, post a large sign with the quote written on it in a key location .

HAPPY THOUGHTS BOX

The first day is also a good day to have the children begin expressing happy thoughts to each other. Cover a box with yellow paper and draw happy faces all over it. Call it the "Happy Thoughts Box." Write the names of the children in your room on separate strips of paper and put them inside the box. You might also paste copies of the children's pictures on the name strips or paste copied pictures of the children on separate cards and put them in the box.

Have the children take turns drawing names from the box. Their instruction is to say a happy thought to the person whose name they draw. Since the children are just getting acquainted, they may feel a bit ill-at-ease. Help them feel more comfortable by offering suggestions for happy thoughts they might say to their new friends. Invite the children to offer other suggestions. Write all the ideas on a large chart with happy faces drawn all around it. Save the chart for use during other happy-thought activities.

SMILE CONTEST

Why not begin the school year by encouraging those ever-contagious smiles. Motivate the children to smile by making sure you're doing a lot of it yourself and by tacking up a few reminders here and there. Here are some examples:

- Smile—You're on Candid Camera!
- Smile—Happy Kids Work Here!
- Smile—You'll Like It!
- It's Your Turn to Smile!
- Have You Had Your Smile Today?
- P.S. Smile!
- Pass It On—Smile!

Another way to motivate smiling is to have your very own "Smile Contest." Begin the contest by eliciting smile categories from the children. (Of course, you already have a few ideas of your own, but theirs may be even better!) Write the smile categories on the board as the children suggest them. Leave the list up for a while so that the children can think of others and add them on their own. A few possibilities include:

- first-tooth-lost-in-class smile
- shiniest-braces smile

- longest smile
- friendliest smile
- best teacher smile
- best bus-driver smile
- most-teeth-missing smile
- widest smile
- cutest smile
- most-often-seen smile
- best smile in another room
- best movie- or TV-star smile

When the children have agreed on the categories for the contest, write each category on a separate library pocket and tack the pockets on a large board with one of the captions listed on page 16. Invite the children to make nominations for each category by writing names on strips of paper and inserting them into the appropriate pockets.

On the day of the official voting, provide each child with a ballot which you have made by making a stencil with a line for each smile category. The winners deserve special recognition. Make copies of the Smile Award below and fill in the blanks for each winner.

OFFICIAL SMILE AWARD

Presented to

_____

For the Smile Category

_____

Presented by

_____

Date

_____

FINDING OUT ABOUT EACH OTHER

As children learn more about each other, they'll feel more comfortable being with each other. The following activities will help children learn more about classmates they really haven't had a chance to get to know yet. The more every child in your class feels accepted, the more your students will feel as if they belong together and that they are, indeed, a class.

MY NEW FRIEND IS...

For this activity have each child choose a classmate he or she does not know very well. Or, if you prefer, have the children draw names from the Happy Thoughts Box (page 15). If a child draws the name of someone he or she knows well, return the name to the box and have the child draw again.

When each child has a partner, have each pair go to a quiet location in the room where they can talk and learn about each other. To help the children begin, provide a few discussion starters, such as, "How many brothers and sisters do you have?" "What is your favorite thing to do at home?" "What is your favorite television program?" "What is your favorite sport?" "What did you do this summer?"

Have a three-minute timer handy. Give one child in each pair three minutes to ask his or her partner questions. At the end of the three-minute period, direct the children to reverse roles and have the other partner do the asking. After six minutes, have all the children return to a circle. Then invite the children, in turn, to introduce their new friends and tell the class all the things they learned about their new friends, thus allowing each child to introduce and be introduced.

Class Roster

You may want to jot down notes about each child as she or he is introduced and compile the notes into a Class Roster. Type the name and description of each child on ditto masters. If you wish, allow the children to draw their pictures next to their names and descriptions. Make copies of all the pages for each child in the class. Staple the pages together to bind them into a Class Roster. Since parents enjoy finding out about their children's classmates, send the book home for parents to read over with their children.

Getting Acquainted

This activity will help children find out about their classmates. Make a copy of the "Getting Acquainted Checklist" on page 19 for each child in your class. During a discussion circle, talk about each of the items on the checklist, pointing out that there is a picture, as well as words, for each item.

Explain that each child's task is to find a different classmate for each category. For instance, each child must find a classmate who has the same color eyes as he or she does. When such a classmate is found, the classmate signs the "My friend" line.

Since many of the checklist items will need discussion time for the children to really learn about each others' interests, this activity will probably take longer than one day. Set aside special times during the day when the children may work on their checklists. You may wish to allow them to work on their checklists during recess and at lunchtime. Tell the children that they are allowed to work on the checklists only during the special times you designate.

You may wish to provide an incentive by offering a special prize to the child who first completes the checklist. Point out, however, that each checklist entry will be verified. All the friends whose names appear on the list will be questioned to make sure that each entry is correct.

To be sure that all the children have a chance to make new discoveries about their classmates, allow time for the children to share and compare their completed checklists.

GETTING ACQUAINTED CHECKLIST

1. Whose eyes 👁️ 👁️ are the same color as yours?

My friend _____

2. Who is about the same height as you are?

My friend _____

3. Who has freckles?

My friend _____

4. Who wears glasses?

My friend _____

5. Who has blonde hair?

My friend _____

6. Who has black hair?

My friend _____

7. Who likes to read?

My friend _____

8. Who likes to play baseball?

My friend _____

9. Who likes the same TV show that you do?

My friend _____ show _____

10. Whose favorite color is the same as yours?

My friend _____ color _____

WHAT CAN YOU DO WITH A NAME?

The following activities will help children learn to identify the names of all their classmates.

NAME COLLAGE

Provide the children with an assortment of magazines and newspapers. Have each child find all the letters in his or her name and cut them out separately. Then have all the children paste their letters to spell out their names on a large sheet of butcher paper or construction paper. Hang up the completed Class Name Collage in your room for all to admire.

Names

Fast names,

Short names,

Big names,

Small.

Long names,

Fat names,

Mine's best

of all.

AUTOGRAPH T-SHIRTS

Ask each child to bring a plain t-shirt from home. On the day of the autograph party, in fact, the children may wear their shirts to school. Using permanent marking pens in assorted colors, have the children sign their names on each others' shirts. The autographed shirts may be worn for special class functions or on specially designated "Shirt Days," for example, the first Monday of each month or every Friday.

ALPHABET STITCHERY

Provide each child with a large, blunt needle; yarn in assorted colors; and a six-inch burlap square.

Have the children use a close running stitch to sew around the burlap (about 1½″ from the edge), to prevent fraying. Then have each child use chalk to print his or her initials on the burlap. (Encourage them to use bold, primary letters.) When a child is satisfied with the lettering, have him or her ink it in carefully, using a thin-tipped marking pen. Using a variety of colored yarns, have each child stitch around his or her initials.

Sew the squares together to form an Initial Hanging containing the initials of all the class members. (Consider using a sewing machine to make the hanging more durable.) Make a two inch hem at the top edge of the hanging, insert a wooden dowel, and hang up the finished product.

Chapter Two

A HAPPY PLACE TO BE

Those who believe in our ability do more than stimulate us. They create for us an atmosphere in which it becomes easier for us to succeed.

John Lancaster Spaulding

THE INFECTIOUSNESS OF SMILES

What is more infectious than a child's smile or happy voice? And what is as exhilarating as entering a classroom filled with the joyful ring of children's laughter and the light their smiles radiate? One thing you're sure to notice in such a room is that the happy feeling is contagious. Erika smiles at Johnny; Johnny says something nice to Sally; Sally turns to help Jason; Jason smiles at Brent. The cycle perpetuates itself as Brent smiles at Erika. And what creates all this contagious happiness? An affective environment—a caring place where children are growing and learning together.

Obviously, the facilitator in such an environment is the teacher, the person most directly in contact with the children, the significant other whose attitude controls and contributes to the emotional climate and the atmosphere of the classroom.

The suggestions and activities in this chapter will help you establish an affective environment in your classroom—a place where children will want to be, a place where children can grow in self-esteem.

AFFECTIVE GESTURES

The emotional climate in a classroom has a powerful impact on the affective development of children. Here are a few suggestions for establishing and perpetuating a perceivably caring and positive emotional tone in your classroom.

- Start the year on a positive note by sending a letter to each child which conveys the message: "Welcome! I Can't Wait to Meet You."
- Try to greet your students at the door each day with an *obvious* "I'm-glad-to-see-you" face.
- Make sure the children know that your desk is a place where they can talk and confer with you. Designate a place in the room (a blackboard or a sheet of paper on your desk) where children can schedule conference times with you.
- Consider having at least one conference during the year at each child's home.
- Consider inviting the children to your home.
- Keep in touch with parents via phone calls, home visits, notes, and messages. Consider sending home a weekly stenciled note informing parents about what their children did in class that week and offering suggestions for ways parents might help at home.
- Send special notes and cards to the children often and give out awards and certificates to observe and celebrate the many happenings and accomplishments which deserve recognition throughout the year. Consider duplicating a supply of the cards and certificates on pages 23-28 to have on hand when special moments arise. Some occasions for special notes and awards include:
  —sending get well wishes to a child absent due to sickness
  —thanking a child for helping you in a special way
  —congratulating a child for giving a good report, finishing a book, completing a project
  —welcoming a child back to class after an absence
  —letting a child know you liked his or her ideas that day
  —giving recognition to a child's friendly act
  —welcoming a new student to the class
  —saying, "I'm glad you're in my room"
- Share your feelings with the children. If you're having an off day or aren't feeling too well, let the children know. You might write a "Beware" notice on the chalkboard at the beginning of the day.
- Share other things about yourself, too. If you have a special sharing day, be sure to include yourself. If you have a "V.I.P." or "Person of the Day" board, be sure to put your pictures on it.
- Give the children many opportunities to talk to each other. You might set up a special communication center for the children to use.
- Remember that in order to create a positive classroom atmosphere, you must have a positive attitude. The children will model your example.

HELPING HAND AWARD

Helper _____

Helpee _____

Date _____

WE MISS YOU!

To _____

Get Well Soon and Hurry Back!

From all your friends in _____

Date _____

WELCOME ABOARD!

From _____

Date _____

We're glad you joined us!

A GOOD LUCK WISH FROM US

A Special Good Luck Wish for

_____

From _____

Date _____

We'll miss you! Have fun in your new school.

HAPPY BIRTHDAY!

This is to certify that today,

_____, is a very special day.

It is _____ birthday.

We're glad to know you!

From _____

YOU ARE A SUPER KID!

Presented to _____

By _____

Date _____

STAR AWARD

Awarded to _____

For _____

_____

Authorized Signature _____

Date _____

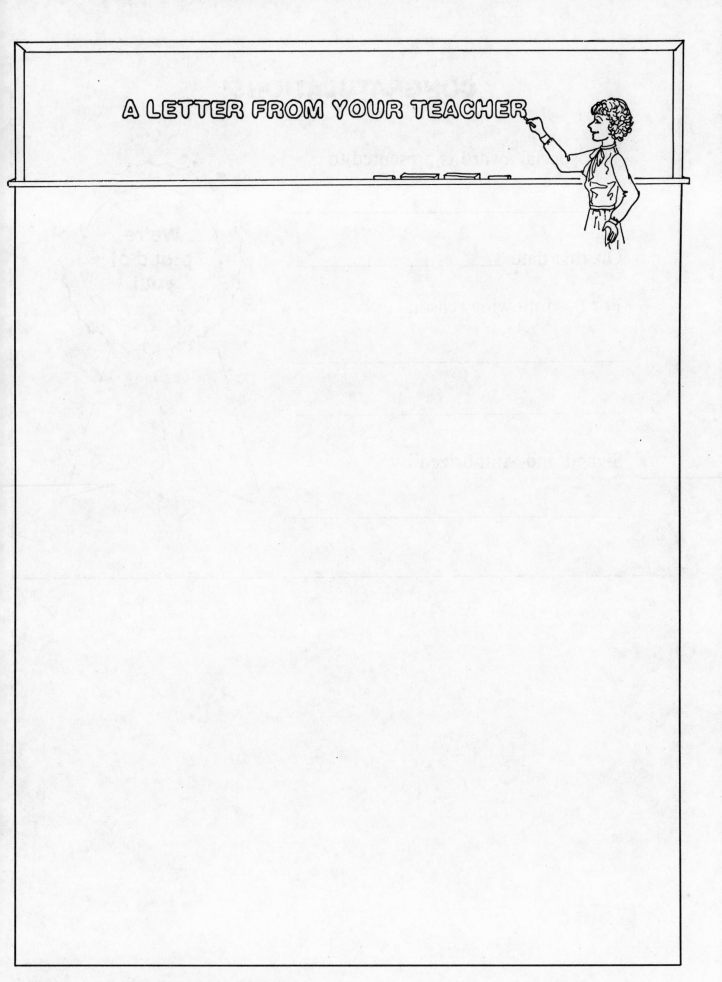

A LETTER FROM YOUR TEACHER

CONGRATULATIONS!

This special award is presented to

_____

On this date _____

For the following reason

_____

_____

Signed and Authorized by

_____

We're proud of you!

Self-Esteem: A Classroom Affair, Volume 2, © 1982.
Permission is given to reproduce this page for student use.

DECORATING THE ROOM

Establishing a secure and comfortable classroom climate is essential to creating an affective environment. For children to feel positively about themselves and others and to act and work positively and cooperatively, they must first feel positively about the place in which they work.

Begin by setting up the classroom with the children in mind. Since you want to convey the message to the children that the classroom is theirs, why not have them help you design and decorate their own environment. Don't overlook including parents in your decorating, too. They can be most helpful in supplying (and building) many of the items you need.

The following activities and suggestions provide opportunities for you and the children to work together to create a caring and warm classroom atmosphere.

HANGINGS AND DIVIDERS

Use child-decorated wall hangings and dividers to both decorate the room colorfully and to divide the room into areas for special purposes and projects.

Weavings   Stitch or tape children's weavings together to make a long wall hanging.

Yarn Stitchery   Have the children make yarn pictures on burlap. Make a hem at the top and run a dowel through it for hanging.

Class Quilt   Stitch children's appliques together. Place a dowel at the top of the hanging and either stitch the material around it or staple the material to the dowel to keep it taut.

Colorful Sheets   Have the children decorate white sheets using felt-pens, permanent markers, fabric crayons (see page 48), or fabric paint (see page 53). You might have them make handprints and/or footprints to personalize a class divider. To make the hanging taut, stitch the top of the sheet around a wooden dowel or staple it to a dowel before hanging.

OTHER DECORATING IDEAS

Curtains   Have the children decorate sheets as above or applique them using material shapes. Hem the tops and bottoms as necessary and hang on inexpensive curtain rods.

Wastebaskets   Have the children make wastebaskets by shellacking torn pieces of colored tissue paper to ice cream cartons. Comic book pictures and snapshots can also be used.

Doors   Cover classroom doors with butcher paper and invite the children to personalize them using felt pens, contact paper cutouts, and yarn pieces dipped in glue.

Plants   Supply soil and seeds and have the children grow green plants in milk cartons for the classroom.

Rugs   Have the children glue or tape carpet samples together on a large piece of material to make soft rugs to sit on for class discussions.

Pillows   Have the children sew pieces of donated material together and stuff them with purchased filler or large rags and towels.

CLASS SPIRIT

Establishing a class spirit and keeping it high will help children feel they belong to a special group and will contribute to a positive, happy classroom atmosphere. The following activities and suggestions will help children develop a good class spirit.

CLASS SHIRTS

Have the class design a class emblem and draw it on plain white paper with fabric crayons. Transfer the emblem (see page 48) onto plain shirts the children bring from home.

CLASS BANNER

Have the children use permanent markers to decorate a sheet or other piece of material showing their class emblem and their initials or names.

CLASS BULLETIN BOARD

Designate a special bulletin board in the room for the children to use to show class happenings.

CLASS MASCOT

Have the children vote on a mascot for the class. Then, as a class, go to the pet store to buy the mascot with class-earned money. (Collecting aluminum cans for recycling and paper drives are great money earners.)

CLASS NEWSPAPER

With the children acting as writers, editors, artists, and distributors, publish a class newspaper to keep everyone informed about special class events and happenings.

ACCENTUATING THE POSITIVE

Encouraging children to develop the habit of saying positive, caring things to each other will contribute to the creation of an affective environment. This is not a habit acquired overnight. However, hearing others make positive statements provides a subtle urge to do the same.

Here are a few helpful hints for helping children establish a pattern of making positive statements.

1. Be sure to make positive statements yourself. Remember that you are the children's model and when they hear you saying, ''You look so nice today'' or ''John, you certainly were a big help today, thank you,'' they will mimic you.
2. Start off each day on a positive note. Children will walk in, feel your positive attitude, and catch it.
3. Continually offer new ways to express positive statements.

- Comment on a child's new way of making a positive statement. ''Monica, I like the way you said that to Jacob. Boys and girls, did you hear what Monica just said? It really was special and must have made Jacob feel good inside. She said....''
- During class discussions, ask children to suggest other ways to express the same idea. ''Josh, you said you liked Willy. What a nice thing to say. Can

anyone give another way to tell someone you like them?''

The following activities include ways for you to encourage children to make positive, caring statements. Remember to be consistent in your encouragement and reinforcement of the children when they say positive and caring things to each other. You may wish to have an ongoing positive-statement activity until making positive, caring statements becomes a way of life in your room.

GREETING CARD CENTER

One way to encourage children's thoughtful gestures toward others is to establish a card center where children can create cards for their classmates and other people important to them. Equip the center with all kinds of card-making materials:

- precut construction-paper card forms in assorted sizes, shapes, and colors
- scraps of construction paper, wallpaper, tissue paper, and gift paper
- decorating materials: glitter, stickers, yarn, doilies, ribbon
- scissors
- paste
- crayons and felt-tipped pens

Emphasize that the purpose of sending a card is to make someone else happy. Talk with the children about messages for their cards other than ''Happy Birthday!'' or ''Happy Holidays!'' Here are a few suggestions:

- Welcome to Our Class
- We'll Miss You
- Sorry You're Sick
- Congratulations
- I'm Sorry
- You're a Special Friend
- Thank You
- Happy Unbirthday
- Just Thinking About You
- Thanks for Helping Me
- Have a Happy Day
- Hope You Feel Better
- I'm Glad I Know You
- Just Because...

PAPER CHAINS

Stock an activity center or other designated area with a large supply of 1″ x 8″ construction-paper strips in assorted colors. Store them in coffee cans, oatmeal cartons, or similar cylindrical containers for easy access. Have a supply of paste on hand. Each time a child hears someone make a positive comment or sees a caring gesture, he or she should write the name of the person and the comment or gesture on one of the strips of paper. Have the children paste the ends of the first strip together to form a ring. Have them pass the next strip through the ring and paste the ends together to begin the chain. Have them continue in this way, adding links to either end of the chain. As the chain grows, the children will have tangible evidence of all their happy, positive statements and caring gestures.

Display the children's paper chains in the classroom. Place them at a height the children can easily reach. Encourage them to continue to add links to the chains regularly.

HAPPY SPHERES

Duplicate a large supply of the pattern below on construction paper of various colors. (It takes 20 circles to make one sphere.)

Tell the children that today they will begin to make Happy Spheres to decorate their classroom. (You may wish to show the children a completed sphere.) Explain that each time they hear someone make a happy, positive comment, they are to write the name of the person who made the comment on a colored circle within the triangle shape. Explain, too, that they will need 20 circles for each sphere they make.

Collect the circles each day and read the names written on them aloud. Have the children who wrote the names tell the class the positive comments that were made. When twenty circles bear names, assemble a sphere and have the children begin collecting circles for the next one.

Follow these steps to assemble a sphere.

1. Have the children help you fold the circles on the triangle lines.
2. Staple the folded edges of five circles together, near the fold lines, as follows: a to a, b to b, c to c, d to d, and e to e.

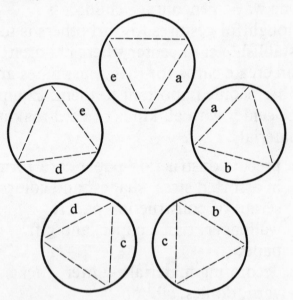

Notice that the top points of the five triangles meet. Your completed sphere will have twelve such intersections.

3. Continue adding circles so that exactly five triangle points meet at each intersection.

Hang the completed spheres by string from the ceiling or light fixtures. These colorful spheres will not only encourage children to make and appreciate positive statements, they will also make attractive additions to your room's decor.

FRIENDLY BUTTONS

Duplicate a supply of the Friendly Button below and place the buttons in a designated, accessible location. Inform the children that you are granting each of them a special, new power. Explain that each time a classmate makes an especially thoughtful or kind statement or gesture, they may award that person a Friendly Button. Show the children how to attach the buttons by using a small piece of tape, folded over and affixed to the back of the button.

At the end of the day, have a Friendly Button meeting of all the class members. Invite the awardees to describe to their classmates how they earned their buttons.

To make sure that all the children receive a button, you may wish to have frequent button days. Be sure to distribute several awards yourself to children who rarely receive the honor.

HANGING THOUGHTS

Hang a clothesline across a window area or from one side of the room to another. Provide several different tagboard patterns of clothes shapes, such as, dresses, shirts, pants, and socks. Also provide an assortment of colored paper, scissors, felt pens, and clothespins.

Tell the children that whenever they hear someone make a happy, positive comment or see someone do a special friendly deed, they may trace around one of the clothes patterns and cut it out. They may then write the friendly doer's name and the statement or deed on the piece of clothing and hang it on the line with a clothespin.

SUNFLOWERS

Have each child cut out a large construction-paper circle and decorate it to make a flower face using crayons and paper scraps. They may add cheeks by smudging pink chalk. Then have them add a long, green construction-paper stem and attach green leaves. Instruct each child to write his or her name on one of the leaves using a dark-colored crayon or felt pen. Pin the flowers to a bulletin board.

Make several large tagboard petal patterns and provide an assortment of colored paper. Explain to the children that when someone makes a positive, caring statement to them or does an especially thoughtful act, they may give special recognition to that classmate by adding a petal to the doer's sunflower. Explain that this is done by tracing around the petal pattern on colored paper; cutting the petal out; writing the comment or act on the petal; and pinning or pasting the petal to the doer's sunflower center.

In no time at all the classroom will be blooming in sunflowers and the children will have proud reminders of their interpersonal successes.

The petals read:
- Thanks for helping me. Brian
- I like the way you played with me. Jennifer
- Thank you for helping me clean up. Ryan
- You made me feel good. Amanda
- Your cookies were really good! Melissa
- Thank you for telling me you like me. John

The leaf reads: Jason

TOWER OF HAPPINESS

Stack two ice cream cartons or boxes on top of each other. Secure them together carefully with tape. Provide an assortment of crayons and felt pens near the tower. As the children see or hear thoughtful statements or gestures, they write the name of the friendly classmate on the tower.

Point out to the children that the tower will grow from all the happy,

positive things being done and said in the room. Explain that they must start at the bottom of the tower and completely cover the first cylinder or box before they can add names to the next level. When the second layer is filled with names, add another level. Tell the children that the tower will continue to grow in this way, until it runs out of room by touching the ceiling. Remind them that the only way it can grow is by happy, supportive things being said and taking place in the room.

FRIENDLY SILHOUETTES

You will need an overhead projector (or other light source) and large sheets of black and white paper for this activity. You may also want to enlist the help of some older helpers for the first step in the project.

Divide the class into groups of from four to six children. Mount black paper on the wall. Have one group of children stand together in front of the projector. Trace around the silhouette formed on the black paper. Have the children in the group cut out the silhouette, write their names near their own heads using white pencil or chalk, and paste the group silhouette on white backing paper. Repeat this procedure for each group of children.

Post the group silhouettes around the room. Each time a child makes a positive, caring statement or performs a friendly act, write the statement or deed under the child's name on the silhouette using white pencil or white ink. Invite the children to point out each others' friendly comments and acts for you to add to the silhouettes.

34

Chapter Three
THE WONDERFUL WORLD OF ME

Selves are not born but made.

Ashley Montagu

WHO AM I?

Every person has an idea of himself or herself as a person. This idea, or self-image, defines how we see ourselves and how we wish to be seen by others. It is almost as if each of us carries a mental photograph of the way we think we should be.

Since self-image guides a child's thinking and behavior, the importance of a positive self-image cannot be overstated. Children's experiences contribute to their mental pictures of themselves and also play an important role in helping children determine how they feel about themselves.

The activities in this chapter use children's experiences to help them learn about themselves and to give them opportunities to think more positively about themselves, thus enhancing their self-images.

CONCEPT CIRCLES

You can use the circle-time technique to help children discover more about themselves—their strengths, feelings, preferences, weaknesses—as well as discovering more about their classmates. During circle time, the children gather in a circle and concentrate their thoughts and activities on one specific idea or concept. Children seem to look forward to circle time, since it is generally a happy occasion when they have a chance to build each other up.

To insure good circle times, establish and explain the following ground rules to the children.

Rule 1   Remain seated in the place you choose.

Sitting in a circle is preferable, since it's informal and helps the children feel more comfortable about speaking in front of the group. Once they have chosen their places, have the children sprinkle a little pretend glue on the floor to remind them not to move around during the discussion.

Rule 2   Make only nice, friendly, true comments.

Rule 3   Talk only when it's your turn.

Use a pass-around prop to remind the group whose turn it is to speak.

Rule 4   Plan your comment or answer during "thinking time."

To move circle discussions along, allow a few minutes early in each session as thinking time.

Rule 5   Put your hands on your head while instructions are given.

This posture helps children concentrate and remember your instructions.

CIRCLE TOPICS

Any of the topics listed below or any of the other topics and ideas in this book may be used for circle-time discussions. Introduce only one main topic for each circle time. For instance, you may wish to have the children discuss things they're proud of. After introducing the topic and giving the children a few minutes of thinking time, invite each child to mention one thing he or she is proud of. As a follow-up activity, pass out copies of the "I'm Proud" sheet on page 37 or the "Collecting Things I'm Good At" sheet on page 38. Each day for a week or so, set aside time for the children to share their sheets, pointing out new entries. Other children may make suggestions about other things they've observed their classmates to be good at; these can be added to the form.

The following circle topics will help develop self-awareness and feelings of self-worth.

- I'm happiest when...
- I feel so mad inside when...
- I wish I could...
- Two of my favorite things are...
- I'd sure like it if...
- I like to be with...
- The best thing about school is...
- If I were a teacher, I'd...
- Sometimes I feel...
- The best thing about home is...
- I like to be with people who...
- Sometimes I get scared when...
- I hate it when...
- I'm really good at...
- It's hard for me when...
- I like to...

(Continued on page 39)

★ ★ ★ ★ I'M PROUD ★ ★ ★ ★

Name _____

Try to think of something you're proud of every day for a week and write it down. Maybe it's something you did or said. Maybe it's something you've been working very hard on.

Monday _____

_____

_____

Tuesday _____

_____

_____

Wednesday _____

_____

_____

Thursday _____

_____

_____

Friday _____

_____

_____

COLLECTING THINGS I'M GOOD AT

Make a picture stamp to show something you're good at. Then tell why you're good at it under the picture.

Name _____

- Something I once did all by myself was...
- I like to think about...
- I love...
- I wish grown-ups would...
- It's easy for me to...
- I wish it were easier for me to...
- I like to hear people tell me...
- My favorite part of the day is...
- I was really sorry I...
- I felt really proud the time I...
- Something I'd like to learn about is...
- I wish I could change...
- The best thing that could happen to me would be...
- I don't like it when people...
- My best friend...
- Right now I feel...
- I'm happy that...
- I wish my parents knew...
- Someday I hope...
- I'm best when...
- I would like to...
- My favorite sport is...
- A funny thing that happened to me once was...
- A part of me that I like is...
- When I'm big, I...
- My favorite color is ____, because...
- If I had a magic carpet, I'd...

KEEPING A JOURNAL

After your class has had several circle-time discussions, you may wish to have the children keep track of their circle thoughts. Duplicate page 40 so that each child has several copies. If you wish, bind the pages together to form a booklet for each child by stapling the pages between construction-paper covers. Following each circle-time discussion, give the children time to write in their journals and review their past journal entries.

MY CIRCLE THOUGHTS

Name: _____ Date: _____

Today we talked about:

_____
_____
_____
_____
_____
_____
_____
_____

My special thoughts are:

_____
_____
_____
_____
_____
_____
_____
_____
_____

HOW DO WE FEEL?

This activity helps children develop self-understanding by giving them opportunities to identify feelings, as well as allowing them to see that others have feelings similar to and different from their own.

FEELINGS THERMOMETER

Give each child a 7″ x 2″ strip of tagboard. Duplicate the faces below, which represent happy, sad, silly, mad, scared, and proud feelings. Have each child paste the faces across the top of the tagboard strip and attach a paper clip to the strip below the faces.

During circle time each day, read one of the following open statements aloud.

- School makes me feel...
- Friends make me feel...
- When I talk in front of the class, I feel...
- During reading I feel...
- During recess I feel...
- When I share, I feel...
- When I'm with my family, I feel...
- When I'm in the dark, I feel...
- When my friend is sick, I feel...
- When no one plays with me, I feel...

Have each child position the paper clip under the face which best represents his or her feelings in the situation posed. Allow the children to show their thermometers to each other. Then distribute copies of the review sheet below for each child to complete.

HOW-DO-WE-FEEL REVIEW

Topic _____

Today's Vote:

Happy ____   Sad ____   Silly ____

Mad ____   Scared ____   Proud ____

Most people in the class felt _____

Reviewer _____ Date _____

INTERVIEWS

This activity helps children develop a sense of identity by giving them some understanding of important past events in their lives. The activity also helps children develop self-confidence in speaking in front of groups.

Begin the project by discussing what an interview is with the class. Encourage the children to watch interviews on television news shows.

MAKING A MICROPHONE

You will need a board about 12″ x 12″ x 2″, a broomstick or wooden dowel, nuts and bolts or nails (optional), a tennis ball (or plastic ball about the same size as a tennis ball), five feet or more of cord or string, and black or silver spray paint.

Drill a hole with the same diameter as the broomstick or dowel in the board. Insert the broomstick or dowel into the hole and secure it with nuts and bolts or nails, if necessary. Cut a hole with the same diameter as the broomstick or dowel in the ball. Fasten one end of the cord inside the ball and place the ball on the broomtick or dowel. Tack the remainder of the cord to the bottom of the microphone platform. Spray the entire microphone with black or silver paint. You now have a permanent microphone for the children to use over and over again in class activities which help develop oral language skills. Keep the microphone in an activity center for the children to use on their own.

CONDUCTING INTERVIEWS

Provide a copy of the Interview sheet on page 43 for each child. You might also make a large chart with the interview questions printed on it and hang it in a place where all the children can read it. If necessary, add drawings to help beginning readers "read" the questions.

Allow frequent opportunities for the children to interview each other (and you!). The children might also take copies of the interview sheet home so that they can interview family members and family members can interview them.

INTERVIEW

Interview someone you'd like to know more about. Write the answers on this form. Also think up three questions of your own to ask the person. Write the questions and the person's answers on the back of this sheet.

Interviewer: _____

Person Interviewed: _____

1. How old are you? _____

2. Where do you live? _____

3. Have you always lived there? _____ If not, where else did you live?

   _____

4. What is your favorite thing to do at home?_____

   _____

5. What is your favorite TV show? _____

6. Why do you like it? _____

   _____

7. What is your favorite thing to eat? _____

8. Where is your favorite place to go? _____

9. Why do you like to go there?_____

   _____

10. If somene didn't know you, what would you tell them you looked like?

   _____

ME VESTS

This activity helps children realize their uniqueness as people and helps them develop a sense of personal pride.

You will need a large, brown grocery bag for each child and an assortment of magazines, glitter, sequins, paper scraps, and other decorating materials.

Follow the steps below to prepare a bag for each child or help the children prepare their own bags.

1. Draw a circle large enough to fit around the child's neck in the center of the bottom of the bag.
2. Draw a straight line from the edge of the bag right up the middle of one side of the bag. Continue this line on the bottom of the bag until it meets the circle.
3. Cut along the straight line and cut out the circle.
4. Draw and then cut out two oval armholes, one on each of the narrow sides of the bag. The holes should be large enough for the child to be able to put his or her arms through them comfortably.
5. Add fringe by cutting two-or-three-inch slashes close together along the bottom of the "vest."
6. Carefully turn the bag inside out so that the inside of the bag becomes the outside of the vest.

The vests are now ready to be decorated. Provide an assortment of paper, magazines, glitter, and other decorating materials. Direct the children to design their vests to show things that are special about themselves. They may represent these things using magazine pictures, cut and pasted paper-scrap pictures, crayon and felt-pen drawings. Some things the children might depict include: family members, pets, a musical instrument played, a favorite place to visit, favorite toys, favorite sports. The important thing is for each child to have a finished product he or she is proud of.

HERE'S LOOKING AT ME

This activity helps children become aware of their own strengths and weaknesses, as well as providing them with the opportunity to think about how they might use their strengths to help others.

Provide a copy of the activity sheet on page 45 for each child. Before the children complete their sheets, talk with them about what strengths and weaknesses are, making sure to point out that no one is good at everything, that everyone has both strengths and weaknesses.

HERE'S LOOKING AT ME

Some things I do well at are:

_____

_____

_____

_____

_____

_____

Some things I'm not so good at or need help doing are:

_____

_____

_____

_____

_____

_____

Some things I could help others with are:

_____

_____

_____

_____

_____

_____

Me _____

CLASS WORLD RECORDS

This activity will help children see that everyone in the room is special and unique in some way.

Talk with the children about the meaning of a "world record." You may wish to use *The Guiness Book of Records* to begin this discussion.

Enlist the help of the class in determining their Class Record categories. Be sure that each child has the option of suggesting at least one category. Some of the categories you might include are:

- most books read (in a given period of time)
- most bounces of a ball in one minute
- fastest runner (for a given distance)
- most baskets made in one minute
- most teeth missing
- most brothers
- most sisters
- most places lived
- longest hair
- highest or lowest singing voice
- most freckles

Hang a clothesline across a window area or from one side of the room to the other. Provide plenty of clothespins and "records" to hang from the line. Make the records by cutting out black construction-paper circles about ten inches in diameter and lighter-colored construction-paper circles about five inches in diameter. Paste the lighter circles in the middle of the black circles and punch a small hole in the middle of each.

Duplicate the Class Record certificate below and keep a supply handy. As a child establishes a record in a category, write his or her name on the "label" on one side of the "record" and the category and class record on the other side. Hang the "record" from the clothesline and present the child with a completed Class Record certificate. Encourage class members to try to break current records. As this happens, add the new record holder's name to the appropriate "record" along with the new class record, and present the child with a completed certificate.

Record Holder _____

Category _____

Class Record _____

Date _____

Official Signature _____

ME PUPPETS

Self-awareness plays an important role in the development of self-image. Me Puppets can be valuable tools in helping children gain insight into their own feelings, in solving in-class dilemmas, and in gaining appreciation for their own physical characteristics. Me Puppets are also highly cherished possessions.

Following are directions for making three different kinds of Me Puppets. To help the children observe themselves objectively, provide hand mirrors or a standing mirror in the classroom. If, in making their puppets, children exaggerate or caricature certain traits, elicit their feelings about those traits. Acknowledge negative feelings and encourage positive ones. Help the children think about changing only what is changeable. For example, a child who wears glasses, but hates them, cannot alter the fact that he or she needs glasses. Yet a child who does not like the way his or her hair looks can try a new style.

FINGER PUPPETS

Give each child a copy of his or her photograph (see page 13 or make photo copies of the individual school snapshots when they come back from the photographer) and a copy of the puppet form below made out of white tagboard or construction paper. Have the children cut out their faces and paste them on their puppets. Then have them use crayons to show hair and clothing. They might also use bric-a-brac and wallpaper scraps to dress their puppets. To protect the puppets from their sure-to-be-frequent use, cover them with clear contact paper. To make their Finger Puppets walk, children can insert their middle and index fingers through the holes near the bottom of the puppets. Keep the puppets handy for use in class problem-solving activities.

FABRIC PUPPETS

Me Fabric Puppets can be made using the outline shape that appears on this page. Make a copy of the outline for each child on drawing paper. Have the children use fabric crayons to draw features like their own in the outline.

Make a cardboard pattern of the outline shape. Have each child trace around the pattern to make two puppet shapes on white or skin-colored material. Then have the children cut out the material shapes.

Older helpers should be available for this next step. Place the fabric-crayon drawing facedown on one of the material puppet shapes. Then, using an iron at medium heat, press the back of the drawing. Be careful not to move the material or the drawing.

Then have the children place the two material puppet shapes back to back and whipstitch around them on the stitch markings (with the aid of an older helper, if necessary). If you prefer, machine stitch the puppets or enlist the help of a volunteer parent to machine stitch the puppets.

Keep the puppets in a special place for the children to use to depict themselves and others as in-class dilemmas develop.

BOX PUPPETS

Ask each child to bring a shoebox with a lid from home. Tape the lids securely shut.

Have the children make the trunks of their puppet bodies by covering the boxes with wallpaper, fabric, or construction paper and by using buttons, rickrack, yarn, cord, fabric and paper scraps, and other bric-a-brac to show clothing.

Next have the children cut strips of skin-colored construction paper to make arms and legs. Have them fold back about one-half inch of each strip and paste the arms and legs to the sides and bottom of the body. Have them cut out paper hands and shoes and paste these to the ends of the arm and leg strips.

To make their puppet heads, first have the children crumple newspaper into a ball about the size of a melon (or a size that looks appropriate when placed on top of the puppet body). Next have them cover the ball completely with skin-colored crepe paper taped securely in place, leaving a "tail" of crepe paper about four inches long. Have the children attach their puppet heads by making a small slit in the top of the body and inserting the four inches of crepe paper into the slit.

Next have the children use paper scraps and buttons to add facial features or have them draw facial features with permanent felt markers. Finally, have them add hair by pasting yarn pieces of the appropriate color to the ball.

Set the puppets on shelves around your room. Bend their knees back and fold their feet up. The finished products will make you think you have doubled the size of your class!

MY LIFE STORY

This activity helps children reflect on their past and begin to understand the sequence of events in their lives.

Introduce the project by encouraging the children to find out about their pasts by interviewing family members. In particular, they should try to learn about one significant event for each year of their lives. If you wish, duplicate the questionnaire on page 51 for the children to take home.

Prepare a strip of tagboard (or other heavy paper) for each child. The strips should be about nine inches wide. The length of each strip will depend on the child's age: you will need six inches for each year of the child's life plus six inches for the cover; for example, thirty-six inches for a five-year old, forty-two inches for a six-year old, and so on.

Distribute the children's strips and help them mark them into six-inch sections. Then have the children fold their strips accordian style (first section forward, next section back, next forward, and so on). The folds will be crisper and more permanent if creased with a ruler. Staple a twenty-inch piece of yarn to the back cover of each child's booklet for a tie.

The children may now make their "Life-Story" booklets. Explain that each section represents one year. Beginning on the inside of the first section, have the children title each section by writing either an age—1 year old, 2 years old, and so on—or the year that they were that age—1978, 1979, and so on. Then have them show pictorial representations (snapshots or drawings) or write short summaries, or both, of the significant events for each year.

When the children complete the interiors of their booklets, have them decorate the covers using self-portraits drawn on skin-colored construction paper, cut out and pasted on decorative backgrounds of each child's own choice.

MY HISTORY

Dear Parent: Please help your child complete this form, giving one significant event for each year of his or her life. Use the back of this sheet if you need more room to write.

Me _____

Year One: _____

This is where I was born: _____

I was born at _____ o'clock a.m./p.m.

The date of my birth is _____

I weighed ____ pounds ____ ounces and was ____ inches long.

My first name means _____

My parents gave me that name because _____

_____

2 Years Old, Year: _____

3 Years Old, Year: _____

4 Years Old, Year: _____

5 Years Old, Year: _____

6 Years Old, Year: _____

7 Years Old, Year: _____

KEEPSAKES OF ME

The following projects help children gain a sense of their own uniqueness, enhance their feelings of self-pride, and provide opportunities for them to experience the joy of giving something special they've made to someone they love.

Before the children present their gifts to the special recipients, they may want to wrap them in handmade wrapping paper and decorate their packages with crepe-paper bows.

HANDPRINT PLAQUES

For this activity, the special materials you need are:

- plaster of paris
- dinner-sized paper plates (preferably those with a "lip" and without plastic coating), one for each child
- mixing bowls and utensils
- tempera paint in assorted colors

Because plaster of paris dries so quickly, have everything ready before you begin and work with only a few children at a time.

Write the name of each child in the group you are working with on the back of a paper plate. Mix a small batch of plaster of paris and swirl a small amount of tempera paint into the plaster. Pour the mixture about one-half inch thick into the paper plates and quickly have each child make an impression of his or her hand in the plaster. Repeat this process for each group of three or four children in your class, varying the color of tempera paint, if you wish.

Punch a hole in the top of each plate about one-half inch from the edge. Direct each child to string a piece of yarn or ribbon through the hole and tie a bow. The children may then decorate their plaques by pasting rickrack around the edge of the plate and drawing borders and designs with permanent felt markers.

Duplicate the poem below or type up and duplicate another poem of your choice and have each child paste a copy of the poem to the back of his or her plaque.

> **This is my handprint**
> **with five fingers as you can see.**
> **My print is very special**
> **because it belongs only to me.**

ME PICTURES

The special materials you need for this project are:

- a small snapshot of each child
- pinking shears
- wooden shower curtain rings, one for each child
- small wood screws with round heads
- felt in various colors
- lengths of narrow ribbon (or yarn)

The rings may be left their original color or painted with colored, enamel spray paint. If you decide to paint the rings, do so before the children begin the project.

Help the children cut circles of colored felt the size of the curtain rings and glue them to the backs of their rings. Then have each child cut his or her snapshot to size and glue it inside the ring frame. Rickrack can be glued around the snapshot to make it stand out. Help each child make a tiny bow to glue to the top of the ring. Screw a small, round-head, wood screw into the back of each child's completed frame.

You may wish to have the children hang their pictures on a bulletin board entitled "Look at Me," so that everyone can enjoy the finished products before they are taken home to be given to someone special.

HANDPRINT POT HOLDERS

The special materials needed for this project are:

- precut 8″ circles of quilted material (solid color on one side, print on the other), one circle for each child
- double-fold bias tape in assorted colors, about 28 inches for each child
- textile paint
- an iron

Pour the textile paint into a shallow container. Working with one child at a time, help the child place his or her hand in the paint, making sure that the entire palm is covered. Press the child's paint-covered hand into the middle of the plain side of a quilted circle. Press along each of the child's fingers to insure a complete handprint. Lift the child's hand off the fabric without

smearing the paint and have the child soak his or her hand in water until it is clean. Repeat this procedure for each of the other children in your class.

Caution   Before beginning this next step, make sure that the following directions agree with those on your can of fabric paint.

When the handprints are dry, set the paint by placing a piece of thin fabric on the handprint and moving a preheated iron (cotton/linen sitting) back and forth evenly over the print for about 30 seconds.

To finish the pot holders, have the children open the bias tape and fold it over the edge of their circles, making a one and one-half inch hanging loop at the top. The children can then whipstitch the bias tape in place, or the tape can be machine sewn in place for more durability.

HELPING CHILDREN FEEL BETTER ABOUT THEMSELVES

Keeping parents informed about what they can do to help their children feel better about themselves can certainly be beneficial. When parents and teachers work together, great dividends can be in store for kids! Consider sending home progress notes telling parents how they can help at home or notes describing changes in a child's behavior. The following letter can be sent to parents offering them suggestions about how they can help enhance their children's self-esteem.

Dear Parents,

Psychologists doing research in the area of children's self-esteem are discovering a strong correlation between self-image and academic success. There are many things that you can do to help your child develop a good self-image and a positive feeling about school. Here are a few ideas:

1. Since children feel more secure when they know a few of their classmates, you might invite one classmate to play at your home with your child. To insure a successful playtime, watch the children closely (from a distance) so that you know when you should take the guest home.

2. Talking in front of groups is difficult for many of us. If you know that a special sharing or report day is coming up, help your child practice at home first. If remembering details is a problem, help your child make a picture or word outline to speak from.

3. Help your child see school progress. When work folders come home, be sure to find a quiet moment for your child to show you the work. Point out any areas of improvement you notice. Your child can then select a few special papers to be pasted in a Work Scrapbook to be reviewed proudly again and again. You may wish to keep all of your child's folders in a special Work-Folder Box. Old papers come in handy during conference times when you are reviewing your child's progress.

4. Awards are so special to children. During the year, our class will be presenting lots of well-deserved certificates. Set aside a special place of honor for your child to display awards and certificates at home. A bulletin board, a scrapbook, or a special drawer are a few places where awards can be kept to be referred to proudly over and over again.

5. A tape recorder can be a valuable tool in helping children see their own growth. Provide your child with a blank tape. Each week or so, your child may record a favorite poem just memorized or read a favorite passage from a book being read. Just watch the expressions of glee when your child compares earlier readings with the latest ones!

Happy Learning!

Chapter Four

THE ALL-ABOUT-ME PROJECT

All that we are is a result of what we have thought.

Buddha

LEARNING ABOUT ME

Each child's self-concept is made of his or her strengths, fears, likes, dislikes, happy moments, traumatic events, and so on. As children gain fuller pictures of themselves, they gain more confidence in their capabilities and they feel better about themselves—they are building good self-concepts.

Since children must value themselves before they can relate positively to one another and can value each other in a way that promotes self-esteem, the activities in this chapter are designed to help children recognize their own uniqueness and find out more about themselves—their physical characteristics, their likes and dislikes, their feelings.

THE ALL-ABOUT-ME PROJECT

Before introducing this project to the children, make the "All-About-Me Box," collect and/or make the materials to be used in the fifteen activities, make the "All-About-Me Activity Envelopes," and duplicate copies of the "All-About-Me Contract (page 58) and the "All-About-Me Certificate" (page 57) for each child in your class.

ALL-ABOUT-ME BOX

Materials

- a large box
- fifteen 9" x 12" envelopes
- plain wrapping paper for covering the box
- multiple construction-paper copies in assorted colors of the "All-About-Me Project" motif
- paste or glue
- scissors
- felt-tipped markers in assorted colors
- props and materials for the "All-About-Me Activities" (see pages 59-64)

Making the Box

Obtain a box large enough to hold fifteen 9" x 12" envelopes filled with activity materials.

Cover the box with plain background paper. Then label the box and decorate it using the project motif, which also appears on the activity envelopes, the contracts, and the certificates.

All-About-Me Activity Envelopes

Duplicate the directions for the fifteen "All-About-Me Activities" (pages 65-80) and paste each set of directions on the front of a 9" x 12" envelope.

Put the appropriate activity props and materials into each envelope. Place large or heavy materials in the activity center near the "All-About-Me Box."

All-About-Me Contract

Duplicate the contract on page 58, providing a contract for each child on which he or she will record the completion of each self-concept activity. As a child completes an activity, he or she colors the motif that corresponds to the number of the activity just completed. The contract then serves as a checklist, allowing each child to know which activities he or she has completed.

All-About-Me Certificates

Duplicate the certificate on page 57. As each child completes all the activities in the project, give him or her a certificate. Encourage the children to take their certificates home to show proudly to family and friends.

INTRODUCING THE PROJECT

When you introduce the project, show the children the "All-About-Me Box" and its contents and explain to the children how they are to use it. Be sure they understand that they do not have to do the activities in order. Then show the children some of the materials in the various envelopes and point out the additional materials in the activity center. Tell the children when they may work on the "All-About-Me Activities."

Next, distribute the contracts and explain that the contract provides a checklist which will show which activities each of them has completed. Tell the children how they are to use the contracts and where they will be kept.

Finally, show the children the "All-About-Me Certificates" and promise that they will each receive a certificate when they complete all fifteen activities.

ALL-ABOUT-ME CERTIFICATE

Congratulations, _____!

You completed the All-About-Me Activities on _____.

These activities helped you learn more about yourself and helped you discover what an extra special person you are.

Signed _____

ALL-ABOUT-ME CONTRACT

I am _____

Color each figure as you finish the activity with that number.

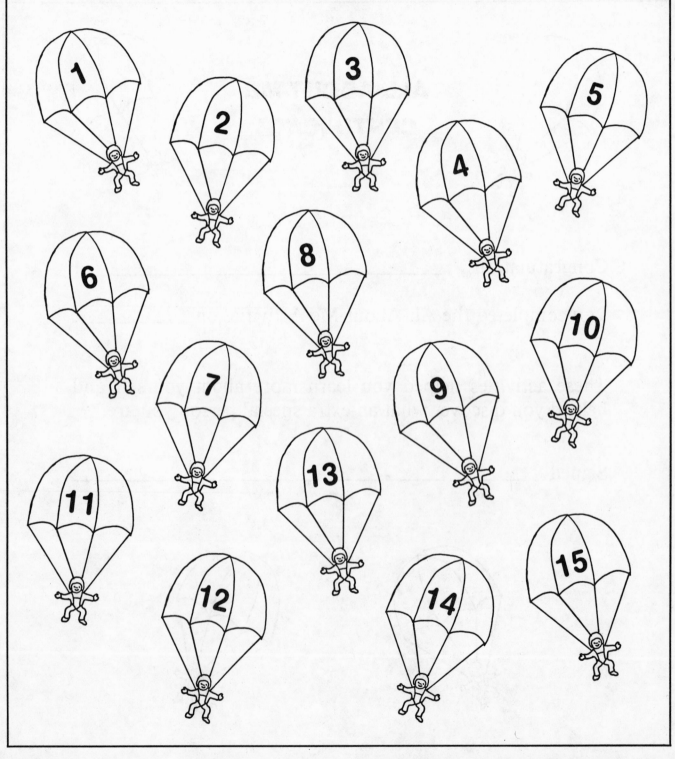

1 FACE MASKS

This activity gives children an opportunity to make masks which look just like them. They can use these masks in plays or for in-class problem-solving activities. Older children may write their own class play and perform it using their masks.

Paste the activity instructions on page 65 on the front of the first envelope and gather the materials.

Materials needed

- a hand mirror
- paper plates, one for each child
- yellow chalk or a yellow pencil
- yarn in hair colors: red, yellow, brown, black
- crayons
- popsicle sticks, one for each child
- glue or paste
- tape
- scissors

---

2 WHAT-I-CAN-DO MOBILE

This activity gives children an opportunity to think about and identify their physical, mental, and social strengths.

Paste the activity directions on page 66 on the front of the second envelope. Make the geometric shape patterns, cut the yarn lengths, and gather the other materials.

Materials needed

- tagboard patterns of various geometric shapes (circles, triangles, rectangles, squares)
- yarn in various colors, cut into 5-inch pieces
- light-colored tagboard or construction paper
- glue or paste
- scissors
- felt-tipped pens
- hole punch
- decorating materials: rickrack, glitter, sequins, ribbon

---

3 MY-FAVORITE-THINGS-TO-DO COLLAGE

This activity gives children an opportunity to think about and identify the things they most enjoy doing.

Paste the activity directions on page 67 on the front of the third envelope. Make large (12″ x 18″ or larger) tagboard patterns of a boy and a girl and gather the other materials.

Materials needed

- large tagboard patterns (12″ x 18″ or larger) of a girl and a boy
- sheets of black construction paper (12″ x 18″ or larger, depending on the size of the patterns), one for each child
- an assortment of magazines and catalogs
- scissors
- paste or glue
- star stickers, three for each child
- writing paper
- felt-tipped pens

4 THE PLACE WHERE I LIVE

This activity gives children the opportunity to describe where they live.

Paste the activity directions on page 68 on the fourth envelope. Make tagboard house and apartment-building patterns, and gather the other materials.

Materials needed

- tagboard house and apartment-building patterns, slightly smaller than 8½ " x 11 "
- construction paper (8½ " x 11 ") in assorted colors
- drawing paper (8½ " x 11 ")
- construction-paper scraps in assorted colors and sizes
- paste or glue
- scissors
- stapler
- crayons and felt-tipped pens

5 THE WISHING CAKE

This activity gives children an opportunity to think about and expresses wishes they have.

Paste the activity directions on page 69 on the front of the fifth envelope. Make a tagboard cake pattern and a tagboard flame pattern. Cut 5 " x 1½ " strips of light-colored construction paper for candles. Gather the other materials.

Materials needed

- tagboard cake pattern
- tagboard flame pattern
- strips (5 " x 1½ ") of light-colored construction paper for candles
- construction paper in pastel colors
- orange construction paper for flames
- scissors
- glue or paste
- crayons
- felt-tipped pens
- decorating materials: construction-paper scraps, glitter, rickrack, wallpaper scraps, decorative stickers

6 HOW I MEASURE UP

This activity gives children an opportunity to discover their measurements.

Paste the activity directions on page 70 on the front of the sixth envelope. Duplicate the worksheet on page 71, making one worksheet for each child. Gather the other materials.

Materials needed

- duplicated How-I-Measure-Up worksheets (page 71), one for each child
- measuring tape
- yardstick

7 MY FAMILY CONSTELLATION

This activity gives children an opportunity to think about their family members and how they are related.

Paste the activity directions on page 72 on the front of the seventh envelope. Make a master with at least fifteen stars, each large enough for the children to write in. Duplicate the stars on yellow construction paper, making at least one sheet for each child. Gather the other materials.

Materials needed

- yellow construction paper sheets of stars, at least one sheet for each child
- large sheets (at least 11″ x 14″) of dark blue construction paper, one sheet for each child
- scissors
- glue or paste
- felt-tipped pens
- glitter
- ruler

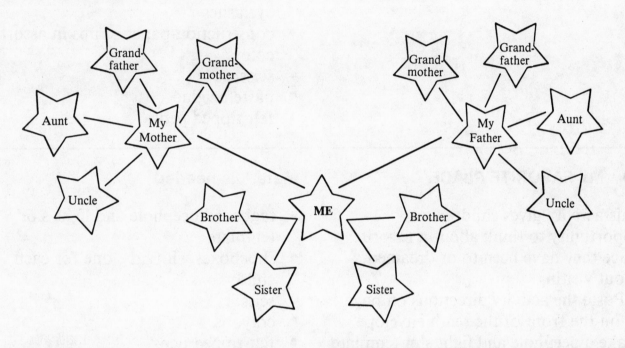

8 ME BANNER

This activity gives children an opportunity to think about and symbolize all the things they are proud of.

Paste the activity directions on page 73 on the front of the eighth envelope. Cut one piece of 20″ x 30″ burlap or felt for each child. Gather the other materials.

Materials needed

- precut pieces of felt or burlap (20″ x 30″), one for each child
- rickrack
- yarn in assorted colors
- tapestry needles
- felt, material, and paper scraps
- sequins and glitter
- paste or glue
- scissors
- hanging devices: clothes hangers, dowels, clothespins, string

9 HAPPINESS FLOWERS

This activity gives children an opportunity to think about and express what makes them happy.

Paste the activity directions on page 74 on the front of the ninth envelope. Make a tagboard circle pattern for the center of the circle and a tagboard petal pattern. Gather the other materials.

Materials needed

- tagboard circle pattern, 6-12 inches in diameter
- tagboard petal pattern
- pink chalk or a pink crayon
- yellow construction paper for the centers of the flowers
- construction paper in various colors for the petals
- green construction paper for leaves and stems
- black construction-paper scraps for eyelashes
- construction-paper scraps in assorted colors
- scissors
- paste or glue
- felt-tipped pens

---

10 MY FAVORITE PLACE

This activity gives children an opportunity to think about a favorite place they have been to or dreamed about visiting.

Paste the activity directions on page 75 on the front of the tenth envelope. Make a peephole and light slot template out of tagboard. Gather the other materials.

An adult or older child should help each child prepare his or her box using the peephole and light slot template. First, the peephole should be made at one end of the box. Next, light slots should be made near the top of the other three sides of the box.

Materials needed

- tagboard peephole and light-slot template
- shoeboxes with lids, one for each child
- scissors
- crayons
- felt-tipped pens
- construction paper
- tempera paint
- brushes
- paste or glue

62

11 MY TIME-LINE SCROLL

This activity gives children an opportunity to think about the important events in their lives and to begin to understand the chronology of these events.

Paste the activity directions on page 76 on the front of the eleventh envelope. Prepare the strips of paper and gather the other materials.

Materials needed

- strips of adding machine tape (25″ long) or strips of butcher paper (3″ x 25″), one strip for each child
- unsharpened pencils, two for each child
- felt-tipped pens in assorted colors
- transparent tape

12 BEHIND CLOSED DOORS

This activity gives children an opportunity to think about and express scary thoughts and how they deal with scary feelings.

Paste the activity directions on page 77 on the front of the twelfth envelope. Make a tagboard door pattern (about 7″ x 10″) and gather the other materials.

Materials needed

- a tagboard door pattern (7″ x 10″)
- brown construction paper (12″ x 16″), one sheet for each child
- white construction paper (12″ x 16″), one sheet for each child
- scissors
- paste or glue
- crayons and felt-tipped pens
- white writing paper

13 MY SPECIAL LOVES

This activity gives children an opportunity to think about the people and things that are special to them.

Paste the activity directions on page 78 on the front of the thirteenth envelope. Make a tagboard pattern of a large heart (about 11 inches from top to bottom) and a tagboard pattern of a smaller heart (about 5 or 6 inches from top to bottom). Cut 36-inch lengths of yarn in assorted colors. Gather the other materials.

Materials needed

- a large tagboard heart pattern (about 11 inches from top to bottom)
- a smaller tagboard heart pattern (about 5 or 6 inches from top to bottom)
- 36-inch lengths of yarn in assorted colors, two for each child
- scissors
- hole punch
- construction paper
- decorating materials: glitter, wallpaper and construction-paper scraps, rickrack, decorative stickers
- crayons
- felt-tipped pens
- paste or glue

14 MY DIARY

This activity gives children an opportunity to record the events and feelings they experience every day for a week.

Paste the activity directions on page 79 on the front of the fourteenth envelope and gather the materials.

Materials needed

- stapler
- plastic tape (3 inches wide) in assorted colores
- writing paper (8½″ x 11″), seven sheets for each child
- cover materials: wallpaper, gift wrap, material, colored paper
- scissors
- decorating materials: glitter, sequins, rickrack
- felt-tipped pens and crayons

---

15 MY WORRY BEE

This activity gives children an opportunity to think about and express things that worry them.

Paste the activity directions on page 80 on the front of the fifteenth envelope. Make a tagboard bee pattern (about 9″ x 12″) and a tagboard wing pattern. Cut strips of yellow construction paper (about 9″ x 1½″). Gather the other materials.

Materials needed

- a tagboard bee pattern (about 9″ x 12″)
- a tagboard wing pattern
- precut strips of yellow construction paper (about 9″ x 1½″)
- black construction paper (about 9″ x 12″), one sheet for each child
- white construction paper
- yellow construction-paper scraps
- paste or glue
- scissors
- black felt-tipped pens

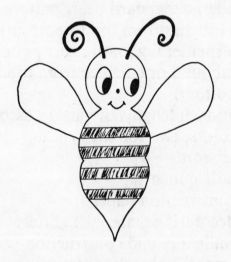

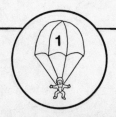

FACE MASKS

1. Look at yourself in the mirror. What color are your eyes and hair? Do you have freckles? Do you wear glasses? Do you have any teeth missing?

2. Use yellow chalk or a yellow pencil to draw your eyes, nose, and mouth lightly on a paper plate.

3. Make the plate the color of your skin. Peel the paper off a crayon the same color as your skin and color using the side of the crayon.

4. Color your eyes, nose, and mouth. If you have freckles or wear glasses, be sure to draw them, too.

5. Choose yarn that is the same color as your hair. Glue pieces of the yarn along the top and sides of the plate to make hair like yours.

6. Tape a popsicle stick to the bottom of the plate. You now have a mask to hold up in front of your face that looks just like you.

7. When you finish your mask, put everything you used back where you found it. Then color the figure for Activity 1 on your contract.

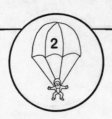

WHAT-I-CAN-DO MOBILE

1. Think about yourself. What things are you good at? Make a list. Some of the things you might name are:

- how you're a good friend
- how you help at home
- a sport you're good at
- a musical instrument you play
- the subjects you do well in at school

2. Trace around the shape patterns on light-colored paper. Make one shape for each thing on your list.

3. Cut out the shapes.

4. On each shape, draw a picture of one of the things you do well.

5. On the back of each drawing, briefly tell what the picture is about.

6. Decorate your shapes.

7. Punch a hole in the top and bottom of each shape.

8. Take one piece of yarn for each shape you made.

9. Tie the shapes together by stringing pieces of yarn through the holes. Tie a knot at each hole.

10. Hang your mobile up.

11. When you finish your mobile, put everything you used back where you found it. Then color the figure for Activity 2 on your contract.

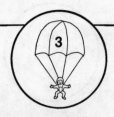

MY-FAVORITE-THINGS-TO-DO COLLAGE

1. Think about yourself. What do you like to do? Look through some magazines and catalogs. Each time you find a picture of something you like to do, cut it out.

2. Trace around the boy or girl pattern on a big sheet of black construction paper. Cut it out.

3. Paste the pictures of things you like to do on the shape.

4. Look carefully at all your pictures. Which three things are your favorite things to do? Take three star stickers and put them on those pictures.

5. Write your name and a few sentences about what you like to do most and why on a sheet of paper. Paste this sheet on the back of the shape.

6. When you finish your collage, put everything you used back where you found it. Then color the figure for Activity 3 on your contract.

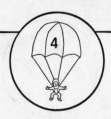

THE PLACE WHERE I LIVE

1. Choose construction paper that is about the same color as your house or apartment building. Take two sheets.

2. Trace around the house or apartment-building pattern on both sheets of construction paper. Cut out the two shapes.

3. Trace around the pattern on drawing paper. Make one shape for each room in your house or apartment. Cut them out.

4. Carefully staple the drawing-paper shapes between the construction-paper shapes.

5. Decorate your cover with crayons or felt pens. Make it look like the outside of the place where you live. Glue construction-paper scraps to show the roof, chimney, doors, and windows.

6. Think about the way the inside of your house or apartment looks. Draw a different room on each page of your book.

7. On the back of each page, tell briefly about the room. Which room is it? What do you like about the room? Which is your favorite room?

8. When you finish your house booklet, put everything you used back where you found it. Then color the figure for Activity 4 on your contract.

Self-Esteem: A Classroom Affair, Volume 2, © 1982.

THE WISHING CAKE

1. Trace around the cake pattern on a piece of colored construction paper. Cut the cake out.

2. Decorate your cake with crayons or felt pens, glitter, and construction-paper scraps.

3. Take one paper-strip candle for each year of your age.

4. Trace around the flame pattern on orange construction paper. Make one flame for each candle. Cut out the flames.

5. Paste one flame to each candle.

6. Now think carefully. If you could have one wish for each candle on your cake, what would you wish for? Think about something you'd like to have, some place you'd like to go, something you'd like to change, something you wish would happen at school or at home. Write one wish on each candle.

7. Paste the candles on your cake.

8. When you finish your cake, put everything you used back where you found it. Then color the figure for Activity 5 on your contract.

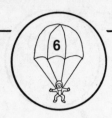

HOW I MEASURE UP

1. Take one worksheet. Write your name at the top.

2. Use a yardstick or measuring tape to measure each part of your body named on the worksheet. Write your answers on the lines.

3. When you finish your worksheet, put everything you used back where you found it. Then color the figure for Activity 6 on your contract.

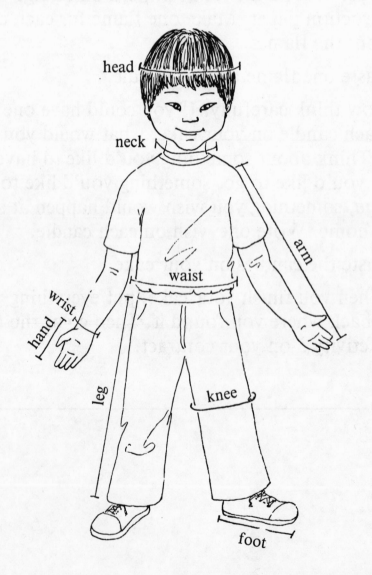

HOW I MEASURE UP

Name _____

1. I am this tall: _____

2. The distance around my head is _____

3. The distance around my neck is _____

4. My hand is this long: _____

5. My foot is this long: _____

6. The distance around my waist is _____

7. The distance around my knee is _____

8. The distance around my wrist is _____

9. My big toe is this long: _____

10. My thumb is this long: _____

11. My arm is this long: _____

12. My leg is this long: _____

13. The longest part of me is _____

14. The shortest part of me is _____

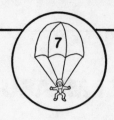

MY FAMILY CONSTELLATION

1. Think about your family. Who are the important family members? How are they related to each other?

2. Take a sheet of yellow stars. Cut out one star for each important family member. Remember to cut out one for you, too.

3. Write the name of one important family member on each star. Tell if that person is your mother, your father, your sister, your brother, your grandmother, your grandfather, your aunt, your uncle.

4. Place the stars carefully on dark blue construction paper to show how the family members are related to each other. Have an adult check your constellation. Paste the stars down.

5. Use a ruler to help you draw straight lines to show how the family members are related.

6. Decorate your own star with glitter. You are the most special family member!

7. When you finish your constellation, put everything you used back where you found it. Then color the figure for Activity 7 on your contract.

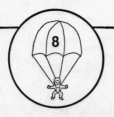

ME BANNER

1. Think about the things you're proud of. Write these ideas on paper.

2. You are going to make a banner to display the things you're proud of. You can also display pins, ribbons, and badges you earn on it. Take a large piece of material and decorate the edges with rickrack or make running stitches around the edge with yarn.

3. Take a small piece of felt or other material. Cut out your initials. Paste them on your banner.

4. Now make pictures or shapes from felt, material, or paper to represent all the things you're proud of. Cut them out.

5. Paste all the pictures and shapes on your banner.

6. Hang up your banner proudly using a clothes hanger, a dowel, clothespins, or a piece of yarn or string. Be sure to put it where everyone can see it. Add to it when you collect new things you're proud of.

7. When you finish your banner, put everything you used back where you found it. Then color the figure for Activity 8 on your contract.

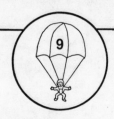

HAPPINESS FLOWERS

1. Trace around the circle pattern on yellow construction paper. Cut it out.

2. Trace around the petal pattern seven or more times on paper of another color. Cut them out.

3. Write your name on one petal.

4. Think about what makes you happy? Whom do you like to be with? What do you like to do? What places do you like to be?

5. Draw or write about each thing that makes you happy on a different petal.

6. Make the yellow center of your flower look like a face. Add eyes, a nose, and a mouth using felt pens or paper scraps. Cut eyelashes from black construction paper and glue them on. Make cheeks by drawing round balls using a pink crayon or pink chalk.

7. Paste each petal to the circle.

8. Make leaves and a stem from green construction paper. Paste them in place.

9. Tack your flower to the bulletin board.

10. When you finish your flower, put everything you used back where you found it. Then color the figure for Activity 9 on your contract.

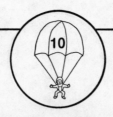

MY FAVORITE PLACE

1. Think about a place you have been that you like more than any other place or a place you've dreamed about going to. What does it look like? Who was there with you? Who would you take there with you? What things are there?

2. You are going to make a scene of this place in a shoebox. First have someone older help you prepare your box.

3. Then color or paint the inside of your box to show the background of your place.

4. Next make small figures that will fit inside the box of all the people and things that are there. Remember to make a figure of yourself. Color the figures.

5. Cut the figures out. Be sure to leave some extra paper at the bottom of each figure. Fold this extra paper back. Stand the figures inside the box and paste or tape them in place.

6. Put the lid on the box and peep inside.

7. When you finish your box, put everything you used back where you found it. Then color the figure for Activity 10.

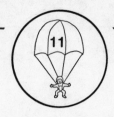

MY TIME-LINE SCROLL

1. Think about the events in your life. Talk to your Mom or Dad to help you remember all the important things that have happened to you. Some things to think about are:

- when and where you were born
- when you first crawled
- your first day at school
- a new house
- when you took your first step
- a new pet
- a baby brother or sister
- a special birthday party

2. Write the important events on a piece of paper. Now number them in order. Which happened first, second, third, fourth?

3. Draw a picture of each important event in the order it happened on a long strip of paper.

4. Write how old you were under each event.

5. Roll one end of the strip of paper around a pencil and tape it in place. Roll the other end around another pencil and tape it in place. Now you have a scroll which shows the important events in your life in order.

6. When you finish your scroll, put everything you used back where you found it. Then color the figure for Activity 11 on your contract.

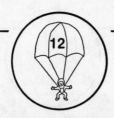

BEHIND CLOSED DOORS

1. Take a sheet of brown paper. Trace around the door pattern in the middle of your brown paper.

2. Cut along the bottom, one side, and the top of your door. Fold the door back. Now you can open and close your door.

3. Take a sheet of white paper. Put your brown paper on the white paper so that the edges match. Paste the brown paper in place. BE CAREFUL NOT TO PASTE YOUR DOOR CLOSED.

4. Think about something that is very scary to you. It might be a nightmare you had once, a movie you saw, or a thought you have. Open your door and draw a picture of your scary thought on the white paper inside the door.

5. Close the door tightly. Decorate the door. Don't forget the doorknob.

6. Now think about your scary thought again. Then think about what you do to make the scary thought go away or to make yourself feel better. Write these thoughts on writing paper. Paste the paper to the inside of the door.

7. When you have finished making your door, put everything you used back where you found it. Then color the figure for Activity 12 on your contract.

MY SPECIAL LOVES

1. Trace around the large heart pattern on two pieces of construction paper. Cut out the two large hearts.

2. Trace around the smaller heart pattern on a large sheet of light-colored construction paper. Make five to ten smaller hearts. Cut them out and put them aside.

3. Carefully hold the two large hearts together. Punch holes along the sides of the hearts. The holes should be about one inch apart. Do not punch holes across the top of the heart. You need to leave an opening large enough for the smaller hearts to fit through.

4. Take two pieces of yarn. String the yarn through the top hole on one side of the large hearts and tie a knot. Lace the two hearts together. Tie a knot at the last hole.

5. Decorate your heart with crayons or felt pens, glitter, wallpaper, and construction-paper scraps.

6. On each of the smaller hearts draw or write about someone or something that you love or think is very, very special.

7. Put all the smaller hearts inside the big heart.

8. When you finish your heart, put everything you used back where you found it. Then color the figure for Activity 13 on your contract.

MY DIARY

1. Take seven pieces of white paper and put them in a neat pile.

2. Staple the pages together in three places near the edge of one of the long sides.

3. Cut a cover for your book from wallpaper, gift wrap, material, or colored paper. Make the cover big enough so that you can wrap it around the stapled edge of your book to make both a front and a back cover.

4. Decorate your cover.

5. Wrap the cover around the stapled edge of your book. Staple the cover in place. Use three staples along the same edge that your stapled before.

6. Trim the cover, so that it is the same size as your book.

7. Cut a strip of colored plastic tape the same length as your book. Fold the strip lengthwise to cover the staples on both the front and back of your book.

8. Write or draw in your diary every day for a week. Show or tell about what you did that day, what you wished had happened, someone you were with, something you did, how you would have changed the day, what you plan to do tomorrow, or anything else you'd like to remember about the day. Remember to put the date on each page as you draw or write.

9. When you finish making your diary, put everything you used back where you found it. Then color the figure for Activity 14 on your contract.

MY WORRY BEE

1. Trace the bee pattern on black construction paper. Cut the bee's body out.

2. Trace the wing pattern on white construction paper. Make two wings. Cut them out.

3. Paste the wings to the bee's body.

4. Cut two thin strips of black construction paper for antennas. Curl them on a pencil. Then paste them to the bee's head.

5. Make the bee's eyes, nose, and mouth from yellow construction paper. Paste them on the bee's face.

6. Now think carefully about things that bother you or make you worry. What are they? Write each thing that worries you on a yellow strip of paper. Use a black felt pen.

7. Paste the stripes on the bee's body.

8. When you finish your bee, put everything you used back where you found it. Then color the figure for Activity 15 on your contract.

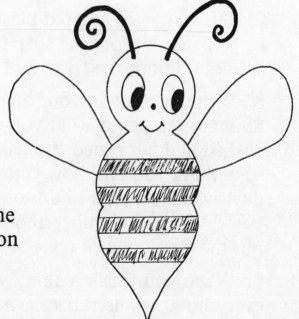

Self-Esteem: A Classroom Affair, Volume 2, © 1982.
Permission is given to reproduce this page for student use.

Chapter Five
MY FRIENDS AND I

*When two people are friends,
even water is sweet.*

Czech Proverb

FRIENDSHIPS

Friends play a vital role in every child's life. Each friendship is different and each provides a valuable psychological lesson. By exploring relationships, children learn more about themselves and their own growth, as well as learning more about other children and how they handle their successes and failures.

Each new relationship enlarges a child's world picture. As children interact with friends and share their friends' personal experiences, their worlds expand and their horizons broaden. Their perceptions of the world are no longer limited to those based only on their own personal experiences.

SHOW AND TELL A FRIEND

Discuss with the children the things that are most valuable to them. After they have offered a few suggestions, ask them if they think that all valuable things can be bought with money. Ask what things special to them cannot be bought with money. Lead the children to the issue of the value of friends. At this point, you may wish to ask them what is valuable or special about a friend. Write their answers on the chalkboard or on a large chart to be referred to during other friendship activities.

Inform the children that next week (specify a date and time), they will have a chance to share their valuable friends with one another. Explain that not all friends need be classmates. Ask the children to give examples of friends that are not classmates, such as, parents, teachers, a pet, a neighbor, a special adult. When sharing day comes, each child should bring his or her friend (if possible) or a photograph or drawing of him or her to school and explain to the rest of the class why the person is a special and valuable friend.

FRIEND PALS

Children should be aware that not all friends are close by, that some, in fact, live far away. Invite the children to tell about friends who live far away.

Children can also become acquainted with new faraway friends through the mail by joining a friendship club. For a small membership fee ($2-$3), the club provides each member with the name

and address of an international friend. One such club is:

International Friendship League
40 Mount Vernon Street
Boston, MA 02108

FRIENDLY DEED COUPONS

This activity gives children the opportunity to practice doing friendly deeds.

To begin the activity, hold a discussion circle, asking the children to tell what they think a friendly deed is. To help them get started, you may wish to provide a few examples, such as:

- helping a friend clean up
- remembering to do your chores without being told
- sharing your lunch with a friend who forgot his or hers
- being quiet when someone has a headache or is not feeling well

Make several copies of the coupon on page 83 for each child. If you wish, make coupon booklets by stapling the coupons between construction paper covers.

Distribute the coupons or coupon booklets. Encourage the children to think about the friendly deeds they will do and to decide for whom they will do each deed. Each time a child decides on a deed, he or she should write the deed and the name of the recipient on a coupon. You may wish to have daily discussion circles to encourage the children to fill out their coupons, as well as to have them offer other suggestions for friendly deeds to be considered. When the children have

❧❧❧❧ FRIENDLY DEED COUPON ❧❧❧❧

This coupon certifies that I will do this friendly deed:

_____

_____

for _____ on _____

Signed _____

---

filled out all their coupons, invite them to share their plans with each other.

It is important for the children to discuss the effects their friendly deeds have on others. As the children carry out their plans, be sure to allow time for them to share their experiences and tell about the reactions other people had when they discovered a friendly deed being done.

MAIL CALL

This activity gives each child in the class an opportunity to be the center of attention for a day and to receive happy greetings from his or her classmates.

To prepare for the activity, make a Mail Bag from material. Lace cording through the top which can be pulled to open and shut the bag. Next, list the name of every child in your class on a large chart.

Explain to the children that each of them will have a special day in the order that their names appear on the chart.

Celebrate the arrival of each child's special day by writing a message, such as, "Hooray, Hooray, it's Johnny's day," on the chalkboard.

On each child's special day, gather the class for a discussion circle. Invite each child to offer a personal greeting to the Child of the Day or to tell why he or she is a special friend. They may also wish to tell about a friendly deed the Child of the Day has done or a special quality he or she possesses.

Then have the children return to their seats to write individual, private messages to their friend. If you wish, duplicate the "Friendly Letter" stationery on page 88 for the children to use. Have the children put their completed letters in the Mail Bag for the Child of the Day to take home to read over and over again and to share with his or her family. Remind the child to bring the empty bag back to school the next day so that it can be used by the next special classmate.

As you can imagine, Mail Call will be an extra special time for every child.

BIOGRAPHY OF A FRIEND

Duplicate the instruction sheet below, making one copy for each child. Following a discussion about what biographies are, assign each child one friend in the class about whom to write a biography.

When the children complete their biographies, provide opportunities for them to share their work with each other.

BIOGRAPHY OF A FRIEND

Write the story of one of your friend's lives. Learn as much as you can about your friend. Be sure to include:

- the name of your friend
- the age of your friend
- your friend's birthday
- your friend's address
- a description of your friend (height, eye color, hair color)
- the number of people in your friend's family
- things you're friend likes to do
- why you like your friend
- a picture you drew of your friend

FRIENDSHIP CENTER

Create a Friendship Center to involve children in activities which help them explore friendships and the roles friendships play in their lives. These investigations will also promote friendly relationships within your classroom.

Duplicate the contract on page 86 and the worksheets on pages 87-90. Equip the center with the worksheets, books, and other materials needed for the six activities described below.

Distribute the contracts. Explain to the children that they are to check off each activity on the contract as they complete it. Designate specific times for the children to work on their Friendship Center activities.

RECIPE FOR A FRIEND

The children complete the worksheet on page 87, naming the ingredients in a friend and writing their own recipes for how a friend is made.

FRIENDSHIP CARDS

The children use an assortment of materials—construction paper, wallpaper, gift-wrapping paper, crayons, water colors, felt-tipped pens, pencils—to design and make friendship cards for their special friends.

FRIENDLY LETTERS

Ask each child to bring an envelope and a stamp from home. Keep these in the Friendship Center until they are needed.

Each child, using the stationery on page 88, writes a friendly letter to a special friend of his or her own choice. (If you prefer, each child can draw the name of a classmate from a hat.)

When all the letters are finished, the children address their envelopes, stamp them, and seal their letters inside. Then, as a class, they walk to the nearest mailbox to mail them.

FRIENDLY DEEDS

Using the "My List of Friendly Deeds" worksheet (page 89), the children record each friendly deed they perform during a given period of time. At a later date, the children may discuss their worksheets and tell about their friendly deeds during a special circle time.

FRIENDLY BOOK REPORTS

Put an assortment of books about friends in the Friendship Center. (A selected list of appropriate titles is given on page 98.)

Each child chooses a book he or she would like to read and, after reading the book, completes a "Friendly Book Report" (page 90).

FRIENDLY DEEDS BOOK

Make a Friendly Deeds Book by stapling large sheets of plain paper between construction paper covers. Provide an assortment of magazines and catalogs.

The children look through the magazines and catalogs. Each time they find a picture showing a friendly deed, they cut out the picture and paste it in the Friendly Deeds Book. The pictures can be discussed during future circle times.

FRIENDLY CONTRACT

Check off each activity when you finish it.

_____ 1. What ingredients make a friend?
Write your own Recipe.

_____ 2. Make a special card for a friend.

_____ 3. Bring an envelope and stamp from home. Write a
letter to a friend.

_____ 4. Make a list of your friendly deeds. Circle the
one you think is the most special.

_____ 5. Read a book about friends. Complete a
Friendly Book Report to tell about the book.

_____ 6. Find pictures of friendly deeds. Cut them out
and paste them in the Friendly Deeds Book.

Signed _____

RECIPE FOR A FRIEND

From the file of _____

Ingredients

_____
_ _
_____
_ _
_____
_ _
_____
_ _
_____

Recipe

_____
_ _
_____
_ _
_____
_ _ _ _ _ _ _ _ _ _ _ _ _ _ _ _ _
_____
_ _ _ _ _ _ _ _ _ _ _ _ _ _ _ _ _
_____
_ _ _ _ _ _ _ _ _ _ _ _ _ _ _ _ _
_____
_ _ _ _ _ _ _ _ _ _ _ _ _ _ _ _ _

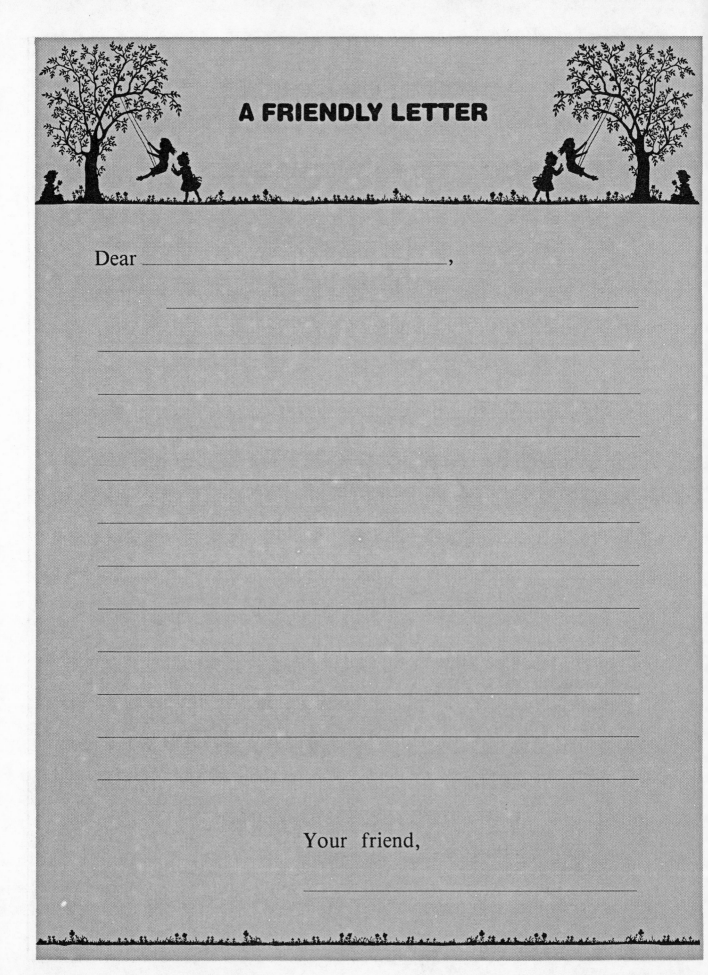

A FRIENDLY LETTER

Dear _____,

_____

_____

_____

_____

_____

_____

_____

_____

_____

Your friend,

_____

MY LIST OF FRIENDLY DEEDS

by _____

Circle your most special friendly deed.

_____
_____
_____
_____
_____
_____
_____
_____
_____
_____
_____
_____
_____
_____
_____
_____
_____
_____
_____
_____
_____
_____
_____
_____

 # FRIENDLY BOOK REPORT

Title: _____

Author: _____

Reviewer: _____

This is a picture of a friendly part in the story.

A friendly character was _____

These are some of the friendly deeds this character did.

_____

_____

_____

_____

_____

_____

_____

_____

FRIENDLY INTERACTION

Children learn to interact with others by being with others. The more cooperative experiences children have, the better they will be at friendship-making. The following activities will help enhance children's interaction skills.

INTERESTS COLLAGE

Provide a large assortment of magazines for the children to look through. Tell the children that each time they find a picture showing something they especially like to do or something they'd really like to have, they are to cut it out.

Place a large sheet of butcher paper in an open work area. When the children have collected their pictures of things meaningful to them, tell them that they are going to use the pictures to make a classroom collage showing all of their interests.

Before the children begin the collage, talk with them about their interests, making the point that even though everyone may have different likes and interests, they can still work comfortably, cooperatively, and happily together. Then have each child choose a place on the butcher paper to arrange and then paste down his or her pictures. Have the children write their names or initials somewhere near their own picture groupings

Hang up the finished collage, so that everyone can "read" about each others' interests. You may wish to have a discussion circle to give each child an opportunity to explain the choice of pictures in his or her grouping and to give all the children another chance to hear about what their friends enjoy the most.

FRIENDSHIP BOARD

Designate a special bulletin board for showing cooperative happenings in your class. Entitle the board "Friends Together." Have the children make self-portraits by drawing their faces and pasting yarn hair on eight-inch circles of skin-colored construction paper. Use the portraits to make a decorative border for the bulletin board.

Periodically, take snapshots of the children working and playing together. Pin these to the board. Have the children take turns writing short descriptions of the photos. Pin each description to the board near its photo.

At the end of the year, compile all the photos and descriptions into a special class book. You'll be surprised at how many children will return the following year to browse through the book or to show it to new friends and classmates.

FRIENDSHIP MURAL

The special materials needed for this activity are:

- fabric crayons
- a large white sheet
- an iron
- large-eyed needles
- embroidery thread or yarn
- spray starch
- material scraps, spray starched and ironed
- pinking shears

Have the children use fabric crayons to draw pictures of themselves on white drawing paper (8½ " x 11 "). Instruct the children to press down when they use the crayons and to fill in their drawings completely so that the finished product will be dark and colorful.

Place each drawing facedown on the sheet and gently iron back and forth until the entire picture is transferred. Then have the children use permanent markers to write their names or initials under their pictures. (Caution: Do not have the children write their names on the drawing paper, as the tranferring process will result in a reversal of the letters.)

When all the pictures have been transferred, the children may decorate their mural. Have them use pinking shears (to prevent fraying) to cut flower centers and petals from felt and materials scraps that have been spray starched and ironed. After the flowers have been pasted to the mural, have the children use a running stitch and green yarn or embroidery thread to make flower stems. They may also add grass using yarn or permanent markers.

Give the mural a decorative border. First fold the edges of the mural over one-half inch and carefully cut small slits along the fold. Then have the children add fringe by tying four or five pieces (5 " to 7 " in length) of brightly colored yarn through each slit. As a final touch, use permanent markers to write a caption, such as, "Friends Are Special Kinds of People," which the class has cooperatively chosen, across the top of the mural.

Hang the mural by stretching it across a wall space and tacking it at the sides. Or, if you prefer, make a hem across the top of the mural and insert a dowel.

FRIENDSHIP BOOK

Tell the children that they are each going to contribute to a Friendship Book which will tell about the meaning and value of friendship. Invite the children to tell what a friend is to them. Ask questions like "What is special about a friend?" and "Why are you glad to have a friend?" to spark the children's ideas.

After the discussion, ask the children to complete the following sentence on scratch paper: A friend is .... Check completed sentences for spelling and grammatical errors. Then distribute sheets of colorful construction paper and have each child copy his or her sentence across the bottom of the sheet using thin-tipped felt pens.

Provide an assortment of magazines for the children to browse through looking for pictures that remind them of friendship. When a child finds a favorite friendship picture, he or she cuts it out and pastes it on his or her book page.

You might also invite the children to draw friendship pictures on drawing paper. Have them paste their drawings on separate sheets of construction paper and add these pages to the book.

Bind all the pages together between two pieces of heavy paper covered with material, wallpaper, or contact paper. Punch two or three holes along one side of the book and tie the pages together using yarn or cord. Use permanent markers to write the title "Our Friendship Book" on the cover. Place the book in a special location, so that children and guests may enjoy it.

FRIENDSHIP POEM

Write the letters in the word *FRIENDSHIP* vertically down one edge of a large sheet of butcher paper. Invite the children to a discussion circle on the topic of friendship. You may wish to use books about friendship (see the list on page 98) and pictures of children involved in acts of friendship as discussion starters.

After the discussion, explain to the children that their task is to think of words beginning with each letter in the word *FRIENDSHIP* which say something about friendship; for example, Fun, Rely, Important. Have the children work on their lists individually, in pairs or small groups, or as a class. After a specified amount of time, have the children offer their suggestions for each letter. Write all the words on the chalkboard or large chart. Then have the class choose the best word for each letter. Write the final words on the butcher paper next to the corresponding letters.

Post the "special poem" where all can see and enjoy it.

FRIENDSHIP WEEK

Friendship is so special! Why not celebrate its specialness with a Friendship Week, devoting each day to a different kind of friendship activity.

To help the children anticipate this eagerly, leave hints about the upcoming festivities, for example:

- Each day for a week or so, write a message such as "Only five more days until Friendship Week" on the blackboard;
- Write "I wonder who your secret pal will be" at the bottom of assignments;
- Make a special display of books about friendship (see page 98 for a list of appropriate titles);
- Change several bulletin boards to reflect friendship themes using captions like "What Is a Friend?" "Happiness Is Having a Good Friend," or "Friends, Friends, Friends."

Monday
SECRET PALS

Begin the activity with a discussion circle, asking the children to tell what they think is special about friends. Also ask them what special things friends do for each other and how another person's friendly deed makes them feel.

Tell the children that each of them is going to be a secret pal to a classmate all during Friendship Week. Explain that a Secret Pal does secret, thoughtful acts and gives homemade gifts in secret. Ask the children to suggest some things a Secret Pal might do. These suggestions might include:
- making drawings
- baking cookies
- designing a special card
- bringing flowers from home
- making a small gift
- sending a friendly message

Tell the children to leave their gifts secretly on their Secret Pal's desk or designate a place for the children to leave and receive their secret gifts and messages.

Write the name of each child in the class on a slip of paper. Fold the slips over and put them in a hat. Pass the hat around and have each child draw a name. Caution the children not to tell anyone whose name they drew. Tell them that they will reveal themselves to their Secret Pals at the end of the week.

Tuesday
FRIEND MOBILES

Begin today's activity by reading the children a book about friendship (a list of appropriate titles appears on page 98). Follow the reading with a discussion of what friendship is—what friends do for each other, how friends act toward each other, how it feels to have a friend, what a friendly deed is, how it feels to do a friendly deed, how it feels to have someone do one for you.

After the discussion, have each child jot down his or her thoughts in answer to the question "What is a friend?"

Provide boy and girl patterns for the children to trace on tagboard or other heavy paper. Have each child cut out the pattern and write his or her thoughts about what a friend is on one side of the figure. Then have each child decorate the other side of the figure to make it look like herself or himself. Provide a variety of materials—crayons, felt-tipped pens, material, wallpaper, construction paper, yarn, rickrack, buttons—for this step in the project.

When the children have completed their figures, punch a hole in the top of each figure and use yarn to hang them from the ceiling, a line, or hangers.

Wednesday
HELPING FRIENDS

Tell the children that for today's friendship activity, they will show their appreciation to all the special school friends who help them each day. Ask the children to name these special helpers and tell why they deserve special recognition for their friendly, helping deeds. List each person the children name on the chalkboard or on a large chart. The list might include:

- custodian(s)
- office personnel
- principal
- vice principal
- bus driver(s)
- nurse
- board members
- teacher(s)
- librarian
- cafeteria personnel
- PTA President
- special helping parents

Assign each child one of the helpers on the list. Then have the children design and make cards, write letters, or draw pictures for their special school helpers.

You might also have the children use fabric paint to make personalized gifts for the special helpers. (See page 53 for complete directions on using fabric paint.) Purchase solid colored aprons and have the children personalize them with their handprints. (Large butcher aprons make excellent barbeque aprons for both men and women; aprons with large pockets and tool loops make excellent gifts for do-it-your-selfers.)

Thursday
FRIENDLY DEEDS TREE

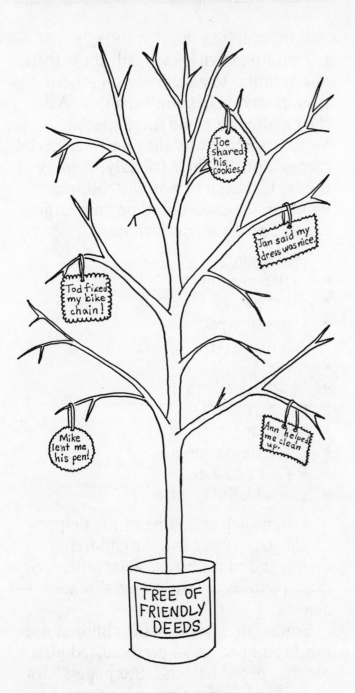

Decorate the outside of the container using construction paper or wallpaper. Place a hole punch and yarn in assorted colors near the tree.

Prepare a supply of construction-paper Friendly Deed cards in assorted colors and shapes. To add variety, scallop the edges of some and use pinking shears to cut out others.

At the beginning of the day, leave several cards on each child's desk. Explain to the children that today is a special day because they will have a chance to acknowledge their classmates' friendly deeds. Tell them that each time someone does a friendly deed for them, they are to write a description of the deed and the name of the friendly classmate on one of their cards. Then they are to punch a hole in the top of the card and use yarn to attach it to the tree. Soon the tree will be blossoming with friendly deeds.

Find a good-sized tree branch and a container (ice cream carton, paint can, plastic pail) large enough for it to stand in. Mix a large batch of plaster of paris in the container and stand the branch in it. You will have to work quickly because the plaster dries quickly.

Friday
FRIENDSHIP PARTY

Culminate Friendship Week with a class Friendship Party. Several days before the party, send a note home with each child telling parents about the party and asking them to send one piece of fruit and one vegetable to class with their child. Explain that the fruit and vegetables will be used in making Friendship Salad and Friendship Soup. As the children bring in their contributions, put them in large bowls for all to see.

On the day of the party, have the children help you with the preparations. You will need to have the following materials available:

- several vegetable peelers
- small knives for chopping and slicing
- an electric stock pot, or a large soup kettle and a heating appliance, such as, a portable stove or an electric hot plate
- large cans of chicken or beef stock
- soup spices
- a bowl (for the fruit)
- large stirring and serving spoons
- a large sheet of butcher paper (for the tablecloth)
- felt-tipped pens
- crayons
- sponges and soap (for cleaning up)
- paper bowls, plates, and napkins
- plastic forks and spoons

Start warming the stock. Have a few children at a time peel and slice or chop the vegetable and piece of fruit they brought in. When the children finish preparing their food, have them put their fruit in the salad bowl, add their vegetables to the stock, and stir the soup gently a few times. Season the soup using spices of your own choice and let everyone enjoy the delicious smells.

As each group of children is preparing fruit and vegetables, have the rest of the class decorate the tablecloth. Put a large sheet of butcher paper in a large, open space. Invite the children to use crayons and felt pens to draw pictures on the tablecloth which show friendly acts and members of the class involved in cooperative work and play activities.

When the food is ready, push tables or desks together and cover them with the decorated tablecloth. Have some children set the table with forks, spoons, plates, bowls, and napkins, while others help you dish out the Friendship Soup and Salad.

Then have everyone sit down to enjoy the marvelous feast they have prepared together. Don't forget to have the Secret Pals reveal themselves sometime during the party.

BOOKS ABOUT FRIENDSHIP

These children's books revolve around the theme of friendship and may be used in friendship center activities and as discussion starters during circle times.

Best Friends by Miriam Cohen (Macmillan, Collier Books, 1973)

Best Friends for Frances by Russell Hoban (Harper & Row, 1969)

A Friend Can Help by Terry Berger (Raintree Publishers, 1974)

A Friend Is Someone Who Likes You by Joan Walsh Anglund (Harcourt Brace Jovanovich, 1958)

Frog and Toad Are Friends by Arnold Lobel (Harper & Row, 1979)

George and Martha by James Marshall (Houghton Mifflin, 1972)

Good, Says Jerome by Lucille Clifton (Dutton, 1973)

It's Mine! by Crosby Bonsall (Harper & Row, 1964)

Love Is a Special Way of Feeling by Joan Walsh Anglund (Harcourt Brace Jovanovich, 1960)

May I Bring a Friend? by Beatrices DeRegniers (Atheneum, 1974)

My Friend Charlie by James Flora (Harcourt Brace Jovanovich, 1964)

My Friend John by Charlotte Zolotow (Harper & Row, 1968)

Nannabah's Friend by Marine Perrine (Houghton Mifflin, 1970)

Rosie and Michael by Judith Viorst (Atheneum, 1974)

Two is a Team by Lorraine Beim & Jerrole Beim (Harcourt Brace Jovanovich, 1945, 1974)

What Color Is Love? by Joan Walsh Anglund (Harcourt Brace Jovanovich, 1966)

The White Marble by Charlotte Zolotow (Abelard-Shuman, 1962)

Will I Have a Friend? by Miriam Cohen (Macmillan, Collier Books, 1971)

Chapter Six
THE ALL-ABOUT-ME-AND-MY-FRIENDS BOOK

You cannot teach people anything.
You can only help them discover it within themselves.

Galileo

CHILDREN AND THEIR FRIENDSHIPS

Relationships play a significant role in the development of self-concept. Every interaction—friendly or not—helps children better understand their social world. Through the feedback they receive from others, children paint a picture of how others perceive them and thus learn to view themselves as others do. Providing children with activities designed to help them think about their interactions with others allows them to form a clearer picture of themselves and a better understanding of the social world in which they live.

This chapter involves the children in writing books about themselves and their friendships. This project actually gives the children an opportunity to think about their feelings, their thoughts, and their hopes concerning the friends they interact with.

WRITING ALL-ABOUT-ME-AND-MY-FRIENDS BOOKS

Before the children begin the project, duplicate page 101 on construction paper of various colors and pages 102-114 on plain white paper, making one copy of each page for every child in your class. Keep each child's cover and duplicated pages in a manilla folder.

Begin the project by enthusiastically announcing to the children that they are going to write books about themselves and their friends. Show the children the folders and explain their use. Tell the children that they will need several days to complete their books and that they will work on only one page at a time. Express interest in reading the books when they are finished.

Show the children several library books. Point out the titles, the names of the authors and illustrators, the publishers' names, and the copyright information. Then distribute the construction-paper book covers (page 101) and have each child print the name of the author (herself or himself), the publisher (the school), and the copyright year on the lines provided. Have the children decorate their covers by drawing pictures of themselves and their friends in the box labeled "The Author and Friends." Or, if you prefer, take snapshots of each child with his or her friends to be pasted in the box.

Show the children samples of dedication pages in several library books. Explain that an author often dedicates a book to someone who is very special to him or her. Hand out copies of the dedication page (page 102). Tell the children that, as authors, they may each choose a person to whom to dedicate their books. After allowing a few minutes for the children to think about their choices, have them complete their dedication pages by writing the person's name and the reason he or she was chosen. Give spelling help where needed. Suggest to the children that they each give a copy of the completed book to the person to whom the book is dedicated.

Introducing no more than one topic per day, have the children complete the interiors of their books. On the day that the children are to write about a particular topic or feeling, consider having a discussion circle (see page 36), on that topic before the children begin to write. You might also want to read a friendship story that relates to the topic to help spark the children's ideas. A few stories about friendships are listed on page 98.

After discussing the topic, give the children the page that correlates with the topic discussed and have them write their completions to the topic sentence starter. Nonwriters can dictate their ideas to an older classroom helper.

At the completion of the writing activity, invite group suggestions for completing the topic sentence and write the suggestions on a large chart or on the blackboard for all to see.

At some point during the project, distribute page 114—the autograph page. Explain to the children that this will be the last page in their friendship books and that it will be a very special page because it will have all their friends' signatures on it. Be sure to allow special designated times for the children to sign each others' autograph pages.

ALL ABOUT ME
AND
MY FRIENDS

THE AUTHOR AND FRIENDS

Author _____

Publisher _____

Copyright _____

DEDICATION

My book is for

_____

because

_____
- - - - - - - - - - - - - - - - - -
_____
_____
- - - - - - - - - - - - - - - - - -
_____
_____
- - - - - - - - - - - - - - - - - -
_____
_____
- - - - - - - - - - - - - - - - - -
_____
_____
- - - - - - - - - - - - - - - - - -

My best friend is

I'm a good friend when

I like my friends because

I could be a
better friend if

My friends think
I'm good at

I make new friends by

The things I look for in a friend are

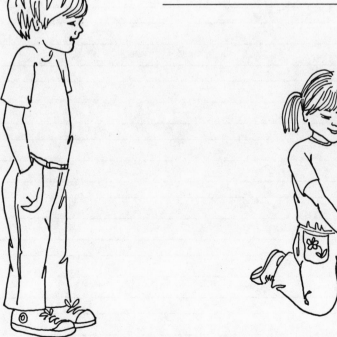

I can tell
that someone
likes me
when

When I'm with my friend I feel

I wish my
friends would

My favorite thing to do
with a friend is

AUTOGRAPHS

**People I can count on
... and who can count on me.**

Chapter Seven
LEARNING TO SOLVE IT TOGETHER

I hear and I forget;
I see and I remember;
I do and I understand.

Chinese Proverb

I CAN DO IT

Each of us is constantly confronted with one kind of a problem or another. Certainly, one of the most frustrating tasks for a teacher or parent is that of dealing with a child who has a problem. Far too often, we find ourselves guilty of a common error—trying to solve our children's difficulties for them. This approach certainly alleviates the tensions of the moment, but think about what it does for the child. By solving a child's problem, we instill the attitude that someone else will always "fix it." Since problems are an inevitable part of life, one of the best things we can do for children is to teach them ways to solve their own problems. If we can convey that there are alternatives and means of coping with frustrations—no matter how big or how small—we've taught our children a most valuable lesson.

The purpose of the activities in this chapter is to improve children's skills in confronting and solving problems, so that when they meet problems in their own lives they will have the confidence to say, "I can solve this myself!"

Use the activities and suggestions in this chapter to fit *your* needs and the needs of *your* students.

115

PROBLEM SOLVING CENTER

You may wish to set up a Problem-Solving Center in your room. A small card file or box labeled "Problems" can be a permanent addition to the center. Compile a list of problems appropriate to the ages of the children you are dealing with. Write each problem on a separate card and put it in the box.

The problems most appropriate to children are those real-life situations that crop up daily. By keeping your eyes and ears open, you will be able to find many situations to add to your card file. Children should also be able to add problems. Designate a special place for the children to write about the problems they see. Transfer the children's descriptions to cards and add them to the card file.

These problem cards have multiple uses. They may be used for group discussion, role playing, group problem-solving tasks, and individual writing assignments.

ROLE PLAYING

Several activities in this chapter suggest that the children role play solutions to problems. Role playing differs from both acting out stories and creative dramatics in that it requires children to think of and act out solutions to problems and to evaluate the solutions. Role playing is a valuable tool for helping children put themselves in the place of another and for helping them

make decisions. Consider the following suggestions for effective role playing.

- Wait until the class members are acquainted and at ease with one another before you introduce role playing.
- Anticipate some self-consciousness (evidenced, perhaps, by giggling and silliness) when you first introduce role playing. Tell the children that you felt awkward the first time you role played, too. Then remind them that the purpose of the activity is to see if their solutions really work and that role playing gives them a chance to test their ideas. In the beginning, ease their discomfort by serving as the warm-up model yourself, demonstrating role-playing techniques.
- Always choose a problem or story situation that is relevant to the children's lives and that has a number of realistic, but not obvious, solutions. Any of the problems in this chapter may be role played.
- Avoid role-playing situations that might invade a child's privacy. When misunderstandings occur or feelings get hurt, be warm, sensitive, and responsive.
- Make sure that the children understand that the purpose of role playing is to find solutions to a given problem and that, therefore, they must deal with the situation as it is rather than changing it in order to create a solution.
- Invite children to volunteer to role play, but only after they have thought of a possible solution.
- Caution children not to hurt one another physically, especially when

role playing situations become highly active.

- Involve the children who are observing the role play by urging them to listen carefully and to ask themselves, "Could that really happen?" "What would I do?" "Is there another way to solve this problem?"
- Stop the role play when personal conflicts arise. Be sure to ask those involved to share their feelings. When an impasse occurs, discontinue the role play and ask if anyone else has an idea he or she wants to try out.
- Stop the role play when the children reach a solution. Discuss the role-played solution with all the children. Invite them to think about the solution's possible consequences. Ask, "Is the solution a good one?" "Why?" "Why not?" Encourage the children to think of and role play other alternatives.
- Conclude the role-playing session by helping the children evaluate their solutions. Ask, "Which is the best solution?" "Which is the worst?" "Why?"
- If a role-playing session is not successful, ask yourself, "Did I acquaint the children well enough with the techniques of role playing?" "Did I describe the dilemma or story situation clearly?" "Did the children have enough time to think of possible solutions before I asked them to volunteer to role play?"

WARM-UPS

A good way to initiate role playing in your classroom is to involve the children in nonverbal warm-ups. Compile a list of warm-up situations (some suggestions are given below) and write each one on a separate card.

- You have peanut butter stuck to the roof of your mouth.
- There's a mosquito in your sleeping bag with you.
- You're at the top of a ladder; the two rungs below you break.
- You try to get on a horse, but it's too tall.
- There is a fly on your nose.
- You're trying to write a letter and your desk is rocking.
- You are fishing and your line is stuck on a rock.
- Your foot is stuck in a hole.
- You can't get your car started.
- Your popcorn popper is popping more corn than the bowl can hold.
- Your key won't fit in the lock.
- Your bike has a flat tire. You're at school.
- Your kite is stuck in a tree.

Have a child choose a card and read the situation (or have it read to him or her). Allow a few minutes of thinking time. You may even want to designate a special place in the room or a particular chair as the "Thinking Spot." When the child has thought of a solution to the problem, have him or her "show" the solution to the class. Repeat this procedure for each child involved in the warm-up.

QUIET PROBLEMS... NO TALKING

Compile a list of problems for which the children can pantomime solutions. These problems should involve more than one person, so that groups of children can work together to solve them. Write each problem on an index card. Here are some sample problems:

- You're in a rowboat with friends. You see a hole in the bottom of the boat. Water is coming in fast.
- You're in an elevator going up to the fifth floor of a building. All of a sudden it stops between the fourth and fifth floors.
- You're in a large store with your mom and a friend. You stop to look at something. When you turn to look for your mom, she's not there. You're lost!
- You're holding your birthday party in the park. When you begin to serve the ice cream and cake, you realize that you do not have enough bowls and spoons.
- You and your friends are jumping rope. All of a sudden two friends near the end of the line start fighting.
- Your very good friend is showing you a new model she just finished making. You drop it accidently and it breaks.
- Some friends are sleeping over at your house. Your parents leave the house for a little while. All of a sudden the lights go out.
- You and your friends walk home after school. You try to get in the front door and find it's locked. You don't have a key.

- You're in class and the teacher is showing a movie. You can't see it very well, since the people in front of you are so big.

Give a problem to a small group of children. As soon as one member of the group thinks of a solution, he or she begins to pantomime the solution and the other members of the group join in. The only rule is: No Talking.

As soon as the "audience" recognizes the solution, stop the pantomime and have another member of the group begin to pantomime another solution. Continue in this way until the group can no longer think of reasonable solutions.

Repeat for other groups and other problems.

PHONE PROBLEMS

For this activity, you'll need a toy telephone and a set of problems whose solutions can be demonstrated using the telephone. If you wish, write each problem on an index card and keep the cards in a box labeled "Phone Problems." Some problems you might use for this activity are:

- You're at home alone with a friend. You think you smell smoke.
- You are sick and you need a doctor. No one else is home.
- Your kitten is stuck in a tree and you can't get her down.
- It's dinner time. Your parents ask you to order a pizza.
- Your sister falls off the fence and hurts her arm. She says she can't move it.
- Your dog gets out and you can't find him.
- You're planning to go to the movies in the afternoon. You don't know what time the movie starts.
- You forget about the bath you started, until you see water seeping out from under the bathroom door.
- Your dog gets bitten on the leg by another dog.
- Your friend leaves her homework at your house.

Working with individuals, small groups, or the entire class, have one child draw a problem card and read it aloud. Then have the child use the toy telephone to show what he or she would do, whom he or she would call, and what he or she would say.

FLANNEL-BOARD PROBLEMS

For this activity, you'll need a flannel board, some flannel-board figures, and a set of problem cards for the children to solve.

If you do not have a flannel board, you can make one easily. Your board may be of the size, shape, and design best suited to the activities for which it will be used. Cut display board, Styrofoam, heavy cardboard, or plywood to the desired size and shape. Cover the board with solid-colored flannel. Depending on the board material, fasten the flannel in place using tacks, glue, tape, or staples.

The flannel-board figures used may be commercially manufactured, teacher made, or made by the children. Pellon is a particulary easy material to use because it sticks to flannel. All the children have to do is trace or draw figures on the pellon and cut them out—they are ready to use. Paper figures with flannel or sandpaper backing can also be used.

Compile a list of problems for the children to solve using the flannel board and figures. If you wish, write each problem on an index card and keep the cards together in a box labeled "Flannel-Board Problems." Some sample problems for this activity are:

- One of your classmates always takes the ball out to recess. You want to take it out this time.
- Your teacher just accused you of cheating on a test. You didn't cheat.
- You find a new ball on your way home. At school the next day, a

classmate says that the ball is hers and that you stole it.

- One of your classmates trips your good friend intentionally. Your friend falls and cuts his leg.
- The principal calls your mom to tell her you can't ride the school bus, because you were seen throwing paper out the window. You didn't do it; it was your friend.
- You can't find your lunch money. You see that Sally has a silver dollar in her hand just like the one you brought to school.
- You're in charge of feeding the class' pet fish. You forget to feed them one day. The next day you find several of the fish dead.

Duplicate the worksheet on page 121. As a child or group of children works on a solution to one of the Flannel-Board problems, the child or group completes the worksheet.

# FLANNEL STORIES

Solve the problem using figures on the flannel board.

Problem Solvers' Names _____

1. Who are the characters in the story?
   _____
   -
   _____

2. What is the problem?
   _____
   -
   _____
   _____
   -
   _____

3. How did you solve the problem?
   _____
   -
   _____
   _____
   _____
   -
   _____

4. Why did you solve it that way?
   _____
   -
   _____
   _____
   _____

SMALL GROUP PROBLEM SOLVING

Since a great part of every person's life involves interaction with others, learning skills for group decision making is a valuable lesson—particularly for children, who rarely have practice in such a process.

The activities in this section involve the children in situations which require group decisions. Before beginning these activities, divide your class into groups of about six children each. Explain to the children that they will work in these groups for special problem-solving activities. Then have each group decide on a name or some other identification for itself and make paper identification badges for each group member. Collect the badges after each problem-solving session and store them for use at the next group session.

Group problem-solving sessions are most successful and effective when they occur no more frequently than once or twice a week and when the children have a limited time to complete the tasks. Most of the activities in this section will take about a half hour in all, but you will want to have a sandtimer displayed where all can see it to regulate the time the groups spend on the individual tasks required within the activities. It is helpful to have the groups practice stopping a task completely when you give the "Time's-Up" signal. You may also wish to give special recognition to the groups that complete the task well and before time is up, as well as to groups that respond immediately to your "Time's-Up" signal.

For each group session, have the children put on their badges. Then assign each group a location in the room as far from the other groups as possible. Encourage the children to work only with the members of their own group and to avoid listening to what other groups are doing. Most of the following group problem-solving activities require some writing. For each such activity assign a secretary in each group to record the group's ideas or have each group choose one of its members to act as secretary. This responsibility should rotate among members of each group. Depending on the ages and abilities of the children in your class, you may find it helpful to have an older child or an adult assigned to each group. These helpers, however, must remember that it is your class members who are practicing problem solving. Their role must be strictly that of facilitator, helping the group keep to the task at hand and aiding with the paper work.

Group Evaluation

Duplicate the "Group Evaluation" sheet on page 123. At the conclusion of each group problem-solving session, have each child complete the questionnaire. (Read the questions aloud for nonreaders and help them indicate their responses.) Save the children's completed questionnaires so that each child can see his or her improvement (or lack thereof). You may even wish to bind each child's sheets into a Self-Evaluation booklet.

GROUP EVALUATION

Name _____

Group _____

Problem _____

Date _____

1. How did you work?

   Well   So-So   Not So Well

2. Did you wait your turn?

   Yes   Sometimes   No

3. Did you help someone?

   Yes   A Little   No

4. Did you help the group?

   Yes   A Little   No

5. Did you like the activity?

   Yes   So-So   No

6. Did you have enough time?

   Yes   No

GROWING SOLUTIONS

This activity gives children an opportunity to see that one problem can have many solutions. You can use this activity over and over again, each time giving the children a different problem.

Choose a problem and write it on eight-inch, construction-paper circles, making one circle for each group. The following situations and those on page 128 are appropriate for this activity.

- Your good friend borrows your library book. When she returns it, several of the pages are torn.
- You accidently trip a classmate. He falls and cuts himself. Before you have a chance to explain, the teacher sends you to the principal.
- You buy your Dad a birthday present. When you get home, you realize that the clerk gave you too much change.

Distribute the circles, giving one to each group. Assign a secretary in each group or have the group members choose one. Read the problem aloud. Tell the groups that they have three minutes to come up with as many ways to solve the problem (solutions) as they can, that all solutions count, and that they are to write each solution on their circles. Encourage team competition among the groups by asking them to see which group can come up with the most solutions. Then start the timer.

When time is up, give the signal and collect the circles. Read the solutions aloud, tallying the number each group thought of on the chalkboard. Discuss the solutions with the class, asking the children to tell whether they think the solution is a good one or not and why they feel that way.

At the end of the activity, pin the circles in a long line to a bulletin board. Make the line look like a caterpillar by adding facial features, a hat, and a bow tie to a circle, using construction paper or felt pens. Add this circle to one end of the caterpillar and pin a caption (such as, ''Growing Solutions'') to the display.

PROBLEM PICTURES

This activity gives children an opportunity to see that there is often more than one way to interpret a given problem.

Find an assortment of pictures showing problem situations. Good sources for these pictures include magazines, coloring books, workbooks, storybooks, and published posters and storyboards developed for problem-solving activities. Mount each picture you choose to the outside of a manilla envelope. Code the pictures using numerals, letters, colors, or stickers.

Have the groups gather in their designated locations. Assign a secretary in each group or have the group members choose one. Give the secretaries a supply of paper. Tell the children that each group will be given a different picture and that they will have a limited time to look at the picture carefully and decide what problem the picture shows. Explain that when the group decides what the problem is, the secretary is to write a description of the problem on a sheet of paper. Remind the groups to write their group's name and the picture's identification code on the papers.

When everyone understands the task, give one envelope to each group and start the timer. When time is up, each group should freeze and each secretary should put the group's answer sheet inside the envelope and fasten the clasp. Each group then passes its envelope to the group on its right, and the process begins again. Continue in this way until every group has interpreted all the problem pictures.

Collect the envelopes and read the descriptions written for each picture to the whole class. Invite the groups to explain the reasons for their interpretations if they are not readily apparent.

SHOPPING SPREE

This activity gives children practice in group decision making.

Have the groups gather in their assigned locations. Provide each group with a store catalog, a sheet of paper, scissors, and paste. Tell the children that each group has $100 to spend buying presents from the catalog for a man, a woman, and a child. Explain that the members of each group must agree on the gift choices and that they may not spend more than $100. Set a generous time limit, so that the children have ample time to become familiar with the contents of their catalogs.

When a group reaches its final decisions, have the group members cut out the pictures of the gifts and their prices and paste them on the sheet of paper. (For younger children, you may wish to eliminate the price factor in this activity and simply have each group choose three gifts—one for a man, one for a woman, and one for a child.)

To conclude the activity, invite the groups to share their decisions and to tell how they arrived at their final gift lists.

NAME THE PET

This activity gives children practice in group decision making.

Have the groups gather in their assigned locations. Display a picture of a pet—a kitten, puppy, bunny, bird, fish. (Stuffed animals and live pets might also be used.) Tell the children that each group will have a limited time to agree on a name for the pet.

When time is up, invite each group to share its final decision and tell how they reached it.

Vary this activity by giving each group a picture of a different animal to name and rotating the pictures until each group has named all the pets.

GROUP BULLETIN BOARDS

This activity gives children an opportunity to make group plans and to work cooperatively to carry them out. Because of the nature of the activity, it is particularly suitable for holiday seasons, but can be used at any time during the year.

Tell the children that their group task this time will be somewhat different from their other group activities and that it will extend over a much greater period of time. Assign each group a bulletin board space or display area (even a shelf or a corner of the room). Explain that each group will choose a theme and then design and decorate a bulletin board with that theme for the entire class to enjoy.

For the first step, choosing the theme, have the groups gather to talk about various themes and then pick one of them. Set a time limit for this task and remind the children that, no matter what theme they eventually choose, everyone in the group should participate in the process.

For the next step, designing the display, provide the children with paper, pencils, and crayons. Have each child design a bulletin board reflecting the theme chosen by his or her group. Set a reasonable time limit for the children to draw their ideas. When the allotted time is up, have the members of each group pool their drawings, discuss the merits of each, and decide among themselves which design they will use for their group bulletin board.

For the last step in this activity, executing the plan, the groups should meet and decide on each member's duties and responsibilities in completing the project. Remind the children that every member must contribute in some way to his or her group's final product. Provide decorating materials and set a generous time limit for the groups to complete their bulletin boards.

OTHER GROUP IDEAS

As children become more skilled at group decision making and group projects, you may wish to try either or both of these projects.

Group Cooking Provide a picture cookbook for each group. The members of the group choose a recipe, assign provision- and utensil-getting responsibilities and cooking duties, and prepare the recipe.

A Group Play The members of each group write, direct, and act in their own play, as well as designing and procuring the costumes and props.

PROBLEM REPORTS

As the children become more skilled in identifying the problems of others and offering alternative solutions to these problems, they will also begin to see not only that they are responsible for their own behavior but also that there are ways to change behavior.

Duplicate the "Problem Report" sheet on page 127 and have a supply available for children to use each time they are involved in those real, day-to-day problems that emerge in the classroom. (Younger children can dictate their answers to the questions to the teacher or to an older classroom helper.)

Save the reports so that each child can refer to his or her behavior records. These reports will also help you evaluate each child's progress and alert you to a child's need for help.

? ? ? ? ? ? PROBLEM REPORT ? ? ? ? ? ?

Filed by _____

Date _____

1. Who was involved? _____

2. Where did it happen? _____

3. Did anyone else see what happened? _____ Who?

_____

4. Tell what happened. _____

_____

5. How do you feel about what happened? _____

_____

6. How do you think the other person feels?_____

_____

Why do you think the person feels that way?_____

_____

7. Name two ways you could have solved the problem
or something you could have done so that it would not have
happened.

_____

_____

AND MORE PROBLEMS

The problem stories below provide opportunities for the children to practice problem-solving skills. Use the problems as your needs and the needs of your students demand. You might consider using the problems in any of the following ways:

1. As additional problems for the activites on pages 118-124;
2. For role playing;
3. For individual assignments. Duplicate the "Great Detective" sheet on page 132, read the problem aloud, and have each child complete the sheet. Or, type each problem on a ditto master, leaving space below the problem for the children to tell how they would solve the problem;
4. As discussion starters. Read the problem aloud; then ask the children:

- Has this ever happen to you?
- How would you feel in this situation?

- What would you do?
- What would be the consequences of that solution? What would happen if you did that?
- What other ways are there to solve this problem?
- What do you think is the best way to solve this problem?
- Is there a way to prevent the problem from happening again? How?

PROBLEM STORIES...WHAT WOULD YOU DO IF...?

- A big bully lives down the block from you. Everyone is afraid of him. At the bus stop each morning, you see him picking on all the little kids and hiding their lunches. At school, the principal comes to your room asking for information. She wants to know why some of the children from your neighborhood are afraid to come to school.
- You are at the fair with your friends and your little brother. Everyone wants to go through the Haunted House, especially you. Your brother is scared; he starts to cry.

- You are walking home with some friends. You have just come from a school festival and it is late at night. One of your friends suggests that everyone take a shortcut across a vacant lot and down a dark alley. You are really afraid to go that way, but you don't want to walk home alone, either. Everyone is already headed toward the path.
- You are at school and you see your friend Sally put the teacher's set of marking pens into her lunch pail. The teacher later asks the class if any one knows what might have happened to the pens.
- You are walking home and see your friend Ben throw a ball right through the neighbor's window. The ball smashes the window into pieces, Ben runs away, and the neighbor runs out of his house and sees you standing there.
- Your class has had a contest all year to see who has the best grades in spelling. The teacher has a special prize for the outstanding speller. So far, you and your friend Erin have the highest grades. During the final test, you see that Erin has written the answers on her hand and is cheating.
- On your way home from school, you go into the toy store with two of your friends. When you come out of the store, you notice that one of your friends has a toy hidden under his jacket. You know he didn't have any money when he went into the store.
- You have just moved into a new neighborhood and you miss all your friends back home. You wish you knew some kids that lived near you. The boy next door invites you to join the secret neighborhood club. You

find out, though, that in order to join and be friends with the group, you'll have to break a neighbor's window. The kids tell you it's all right, because the neighbor is very rich.
- Tonight is one of your best friend's birthday party. Your friend really wants you to be there and you promised you would be. Another good friend calls to tell you she just got tickets to the circus and wants you to go. You've always wanted to see the circus and the tickets are good for only one night, the night of the party.
- You are at school and go to get your bike to ride home. You discover you have a flat tire. You look up and notice that a boy has a sharp stick in his hand and is poking the tire of someone else's bike. You look at your tire and see that it also has a hole in it.

BOOKS FOR PROBLEM SOLVING

Many good books, written for children, deal with solving problems. In each case, the main character is confronted by a problem and must find a way to solve it. These books make excellent discussion topics. Before introducing a book to the class, you will probably find it useful to familiarize yourself with the story and its characters and compile a list of relevant questions. As you read a story to the class, you may wish to stop reading before the character solves the problem to ask the children to: 1) identify the problem,

2) tell what feelings the characters are having, and 3) give a possible solution to the problem. You might also distribute duplicated copies of the "Solution" worksheet on page 131 for the children to complete. Be sure to finish the story and ask the children if they agree with the chosen solution and why (or why not).

The following list offers some suggested books with problem-solving themes.

Annie and the Old One by Misha Miles (Little, Brown and Company, 1971)

Arthur's Honey Bear by Lillian Aberman Hoban (Harper & Row, 1974)

Benjie on His Own by Joan M. Lexau (Dial Press, 1970)

The Blind Colt by Glen Rounds (Holiday House, 1960)

The Boy in the 49th Seat by Florence Hayes (Random House, 1969)

The Boy with a Problem by Joan Fassler (Behavioral Publications, 1971)

The Boy Who Wouldn't Talk by Louis Kalb Bouchard (Doubleday, 1969)

The Bully of Barham Street by Mary Stolz (Harper & Row, 1974)

The Empty Schoolhouse by Natalie Carson (Harper & Row, 1965)

Evan's Corner by Elizabeth Starr Hill (Holt, Rinehart & Winston, 1967)

Goggles by Ezra Jack Keats (Macmillan, 1969)

Grandmother Oma by Ilse Kleberger (Atheneum, 1967)

The Great Hamster Hunt by Lenore Hochman Blegvad and Erick Blegvad (Harcourt Brace Jovanovich, 1969)

The Hating Book by Charlotte Zolotow (Harper & Row, 1969)

Henry and the Clubhouse by Beverly Cleary (William Morrow, 1957)

Henry Reed's Baby-Sitting Service by Keith Robertson (The Biking Press, 1966)

Ira Sleeps Over by Bernard Waber (Houghton Mifflin, 1972)

James the Jaguar by Mary Lystad (G.P. Putnam's Sons, 1972)

Left, Right, Left, Right by Muriel Stanek (Albert Whitman, 1969)

The Little Engine That Could by Watty Piper (Platt & Monk, 1961)

Look Through My Window by Jean Little (Harper & Row, 1965)

Miguel's Mountain by Bill Binzen (Coward, McCann & Geoghegan, 1968)

Miss Suzy's Birthday by Miriam Burt Young (Parent's Magazine Press, 1974)

Nannabah's Friend by Mary Perrine (Houghton Mifflin, 1970)

Only One Ant by Leonore Klein (Hastings House Publishers, 1971)

Pelle's New Suit by Elas Martmas Beskow (Harper & Row, 1929)

Sabrina by Martha G. Alexander (Dial Press, 1971)

Seven Stories for Growth by Daniel Sugarman and Rolaine A Hochstein (Pitman Learning, 1965)

Sidewalk Story by Sharon Bell Mathis (The Biking Press, 1971)

A Small Lot by Eros Keith (Bradbury Press, 1968)

Soo Finds a Way by June York Behrens (Children's Press, 1965)

Susan's Magic by Nan Hayden Agle (The Seabury Press, 1973)

Swimmy by Leo Lionni (Pantheon Books, 1963)

When Carlos Closed the Street by Peggy Mann (Coward, McCann & Geoghegan, 1969)

Where's Al? by Byron Barton (The Seabury Press, 1971)

SOLUTION

Discoverer _____

Discovery Date _____

The problem was:

_____
- -
_____
_____
- -
_____
_____
- -
_____

My solution was:

_____
- -
_____
_____
- -
_____
_____
- -
_____

GREAT DETECTIVE

Detective's Name _____

Date Problem Solved _____

Today's problem was:

_____
- -
_____
_____
- -
_____
_____
- -
_____
_____
- -
_____

I would solve it this way:

_____
- -
_____
_____
- -
_____
_____
- -
_____
_____
- -
_____

Appendix
THE WORLD OF BOOKS

BIBLIOTHERAPY

The multi-faceted problems of adjustment probably provide the greatest challenges children face. It is estimated that at least one out of ten persons will suffer a mental or emotional breakdown during his or her lifetime. Fear, hate, frustration, and prejudice will no doubt plague the other ninety percent at one time or another.

A process developed many years ago to help children deal with problems of adjustment and appropriately called "bibliotherapy" has successfully enhanced the personality development of many children and adolescents. This psychoeducational technique helps children identify with and model the appropriate behavior of real and imaginary characters in books. The scope of bibliotherapy has enhanced the self-concept and academic junctioning of learning disabled as well as gifted children What's more, it's a fun and easy technique that can be employed in the home or classroom!

CHARACTER IDENTIFICATION

Bibliotherapy consists of three stages: identification, catharsis, and insight. Identification is the first and most important stage. It is here that the teacher or parent must use his or her own insight into the student's or child's interests and concerns. The teacher or parent ascertains the personal traits manifested by the characters in the stories and matches them with the child's interests and personality in hope that the child will emulate these traits.

Long before children read easily, they meet problems which should not be tabled for future discussion. Problems such as divorce in the family, the arrival of a new baby, a death, and fears of various types confront many young children. In the preschool years, the first identification in literature usually comes through stories read or told by an older person. The story-listening situation generally encourages a child to view himself or herself as one of the characters in the story and to think accordingly. A story may be repeated many times so that certain parts of the story become fixed or memorized unconsciously. The child integrates the story into his or her actual experience. The stories, in themselves, have no therapeutic value. Children must be given time to ask questions and then be allowed to talk about their feelings, so that any misconceptions can be corrected. Often children will reread the same book, coming back to a story with other questions when they are better able to handle the answers.

Somewhere around the age of six, children begin to read for themselves. Without the intrusion of another person between a child and the ideas, the chances for identification are multiplied. However, there still must be a discussion time to clarify questions and answers. There are also times during the day when identification is fostered by the peer group. This can occur during the sharing and discussion following a reading by the teacher (for all age groups). The impact of identification can be greater when children suddenly find that they are not alone in their concerns, that others in the group share similar concerns and fears.

The *right* book might also be able to innoculate a child against a future trauma. Losing sight of Mommy in a crowded supermarket, for example, may be terrifying for a child. But a story such as Margaret Wise Brown's *The Runaway Bunny,* where a mother rabbit details the lengths to which she would go to find her child, can reassure youngsters that they will not be abandoned.

The correct exposure at the correct time is a key to successful bibliotherapy. Consult with a good reference librarian to assure the correct exposure, provided by the right book. A list of suitable books for all kinds of children's concerns appears at the end of this chapter. There are also lists of many fine books suitable for various adjustment problems which have been prepared by library associations and other professional organizations.

THE ROLE OF ILLUSTRATIONS

The value of bibliotherapy is not limited to an identification with characters in books. Substantial evidence supports the idea that illustrations in books provide an important and effective means of learning facts, attitudes, and values. There are many fine children's books which transmit their messages through their illustrations. The pictures may determine in large measure the concept of self that the viewer constructs. The child who does not even know how to read can be greatly influenced by looking at the pictures.

Illustrations can serve to extend a child's perceptions to worlds beyond his or her own. *The Boy Who Wouldn't Talk* by Lois K. Bouchard with Ann Grifalcon's line and wash drawings, for instance, might help a child realize the difficulties a Puerto Rican boy in New York experiences when he fails to adjust to a new environment in which everyone speaks a language different from his own.

Similar in purpose is the little picture book *My Dog Is Lost* prepared for Puerto Rican children. In it, a lonesome little boy searches for his lost dog on his first day on the streets of New York. A banker, in whose window the child reads a sign in Spanish which announces, "We speak Spanish," gives the boy a placard with "My dog is lost" written on it in English. The child's efforts to describe the dog using Spanish words and accompanying gestures intrigue all those who join the search. The grand climax occurs when his "Perrito" jumps down from behind a mounted policeman who is helping the dog locate its master. This small book by Ezra Jack Keats and Pat Cherr combines many elements that encourage Puerto Rican children to believe they have a place in the sun. A Puerto Rican child will return to the book many times to view the message so vividly portrayed in the illustrations.

EMPATHY THROUGH BOOKS

When young people understand, respect, and admire diversity, they need not fear differences in color, ability, or life situations. Books do not have to preach. But they do have to speak to the conscience, imagination, and heart of a child. Many fine children's books speak with clear and forceful vision. Bibliotherapy offers a vehicle for matching these messages with the needs of children.

Many stories can help instill in children both social awareness and empathy and can give them a better understanding of the limitations many people must live with.

DISABILITIES

So rarely are children given a chance to ask questions about different disabilities, that when they are confronted with a disabled person, they are usually quite uncomfortable. There are numerous book heroes and heroines who have overcome difficulties. These books can serve to inform nonhandicapped children as well as inspire the disabled child.

Though some of the books may be above grade level in readability, the teacher can paraphrase the story for the class. Pictures of the hero or heroine can be shown to the class.

You may wish to combine reading about disabilities with other related activities. Consider devoting a few days or a week to the discussion of disabilities. Spend a part of each day reading and talking about a different kind of disability and the hardships involved. There are a number of good films about disabilities available at county offices of education. You may wish to invite other classes to view the films with you. You may also wish to invite disabled persons from the community to the classroom to tell the children about their disabilities and to convey that although they may look different, they have feelings and thoughts just like everyone else does.

As a follow-up activity, you may wish to visit a center near your school that treats children with particular disabilities. Each child could then write letters or draw pictures for the new friends they made during their visit.

SOCIAL AWARENESS

As with disabilities, books can also help children better understand other problems many people face—loneliness, aging, prejudice, poverty. Consider combining reading about various personal and social ills with other related activities. For example, after reading a book about loneliness or aging, such as *Maxie* by Mildred Kantrowitz, the children might visit an old people's home bringing homemade gifts and cards. After reading a book about poverty, such as *Down, Down, the Mountain* by Ellis Credle, the class might collect toys, food, or clothing for the needy or support a community project for the needy by collecting aluminum cans for recycling. After reading about illness and dying, the children might exchange letters with chronically ill children in a hospital.

BOOKS FOR BIBLIOTHERAPY

Adoption
Abby by Jeanette Caines (Harper & Row, 1973)
Adopted Jane by Helen Daringer (Harcourt, Brace Jovanovich, 1973)

Appearance—Being Plain
The Plain Princess by Phyllis McGinley (Lippincott, 1945)

Appearance—Being Plump
Fat Elliot and the Gorilla by Manus Pinkwater (Scholastic, 1974)

Appearance—Being Small
Smallest Boy in the Class by Jerrold Beim (William Morrow, 1949)

Appearance—Being Tall
Tall Tina by Muriel Stanek (Albert Whitman, 1970)
Very Tall Little Girl by Phyllis Krasilovsky (Doubleday, 1969)

Appearance—Having Freckles
Freckle Juice by Judy Blume (Four Winds Press, 1971)

Appearance—Missing Teeth
Eddie and the Fire Engine by Carolyn Haywood (William Morrow, 1949)

Appearance—Wearing Glasses
Mom I Need Glasses! by Angelika Wolff (Lion Press, 1970)
Spectacles by Ellen Raskin (Atheneum, 1974)

Death and Dying
About Dying: An Open Family Book for Parents and Children Together by Sara Bonnett Stein (Walker & Co., 1974)
Annie and the Old One by Miska Miles (Little Brown, 1971)
Growing Time by Sandol Stoddard Warburg (Houghton Mifflin, 1969)
The Magic Moth by Virginia Lee (The Seabury Press, 1972)
Nana Upstairs and Nana Downstairs by Tomie de Paola (G. P. Putnam's Sons, 1973)
Scat by Arnold Dobrin (Four Winds Press, 1971)
A Taste of Blackberries by Doris Buchanan Smith (Crowell, 1973)
Tenth Good Thing About Barney by Judith Viorst (Atheneum, 1971)
Why Did He Die? by Audrey Harris (Lerner Publications, 1965)

Divorce
Emily and the Klunky Baby and the Next Door Dog by Joan Lexau (Dial Press, 1972)
A Father Like That by Charlotte Zolotow (Harper & Row, 1971)
How Does It Feel When Your Parents Get Divorced? by Terry Berger (Julian Messner, 1977)

Disabilities—Blindness and Deafness
The Child of the Silent Night by Edith Hunter (Houghton Mifflin, 1963)
Lisa and Her Soundless World by Edna S. Levine (Human Sciences Press, 1974)
A Rainbow for Robin by Marguerite Vance (Dutton, 1966)
Seeing Fingers: The Story of Louis Braille by Etaa DeGering (McKay, 1962)
Windows for Rosemary by Marguerite Vance (Dutton, 1956)

Disabilities—Learning
He's My Brother by Joe Lasker (Whitman, 1974)

One Little Girl by Joan Fassler (Human Science Press, 1969)

Disabilities—Physical

Sink It, Rusty by Matt Christopher (Little, Brown, 1963)

Fear—At Night

Bedtime for Frances by Russell C. Hoban (Harper & Row, 1960)

Buster and the Bogeyman by Anne Rockwell *(Four Winds Press, 1978)*

Eugene the Brave by Ellen Conford (Little Brown, 1978)

Ira Sleeps Over by Bernard Waber (Houghton Mifflin, 1972)

One Dragon's Dream by Peter Parey (Bradbury, 1978)

There's a Nightmare in My Closet by Mercer Mayer (Dial Press, 1976)

Fear—Of the Unknown

Things I Hate by Harriet Wittels and Joan Greisman (Behavioral Publications, 1973)

Where the Wild Things Are by Maurice Sendak (Scholastic, 1963)

Going to the Hospital

Curious George Goes to the Hospital by Margaret and H. A. Rey (Houghton Mifflin, 1966)

I Think I will Go to the Hospital by Jean Tamburine (Abingdon Press, 1965)

My Doctor by Harlow Rockwell (Macmillan, 1973)

Jealousy of Siblings

Nobody Asked Me If I Wanted A Baby Sister by Martha Alexander (Dial Press, 1971)

She Came Bringing Me That Little Baby Girl by Eloise Greenfield (Lippincott, 1974)

On Mother's Lap by Ann Scott (McGraw-Hill, 1972)

If It Weren't for You by Charlotte Zolotow (Harper & Row, 1972)

Racial Awareness

Bad Boy, Good Boy by Marie Hall Ets (Crowell, 1967)

The Boy Who Didn't Believe in Spring by Lucille Clifton (E. P. Dutton, 1973)

Bright April by Marguerite De Angeli (Doubleday, 1946)

Fun for Chris by Blossom Randall (Whitman, 1956)

Gilberto and the Wind by Marie Ets (Viking, 1963)

Good, Says Jerome by Lucille Clifton (Dutton, 1973)

The Hundred Dresses by Eleanor Estes (Harcourt Brace Jovanovich, 1972)

My Dog Is Lost by Ezra Keats and Pat Cherr (Crowell, 1960)

Two Is A Team by Lorraine and Jerrold Beim (Harcourt Brace, Jovanovich, 1945, 1974)

Shyness

Benjie by Joan Lexau (Dial Press, 1964)

Crow Boy by Taro Yashima (Viking Press, 1955)

New Boy in School by Mary Justus (Hastings, 1963)

Plenty For Three by Liesel Shorpen (Coward, McCann & Geoghegan, 1971)

Shy Little Girl by Phyllis Krasilovsky (Houghton Mifflin, 1970)

A Tiger Called Thomas by Charlotte Zolotow (Lothrop, Lee and Shepard, 1963)

INDEX